# And Then I Woke Up

To Cindy

Thank You for All that you do with our Chapter! So glad that you are on the OK Board, And even more so, I'm honored to be your friend.

Love You Much

David Shreatt

To Linda,

Thank You for all that you do with our Chapter! So glad that you are on the OK Board, and even more so. I'm honored to be your friend.

Love you Much!

Your friend,

# And Then I Woke Up

FROM SUICIDE TO SUCCESS

• • •

*David Ahmad Threatt*

A portion of proceeds from this book will be donated to The American Foundation for Suicide Prevention. www.afsp.org

The poems throughout the book are poems written by the author, and all were written after his suicide attempt and are shown in italicized print.

Scripture quotations are taken from the *Holy Bible*, and are shown in bold print.

Cover photo courtesy of Rudolph Tolar So Focus Photography.

ISBN-13: 9780692567319
ISBN-10: 0692567313

# NATIONAL SUICIDE PREVENTION LIFELINE™

**1-800-273-TALK (8255)**

suicidepreventionlifeline.org

# Having Trouble Coping?

# Book Review

• • •

"DAVID SHARES HIS EXPERIENCES IN his new memoir, And Then I Woke Up, encouraging others who have struggled to hold on to hope. He makes it clear that the path of resilience can come in the form of mental health treatment, spiritual practice, and other modalities that restore mental health and the human spirit. Speaking out about these lived experiences of suicidal thoughts, behavior, and the process of recovery, is important as societal stigma toward mental  health is diminishing. The voice of lived experience can inspire others and take the stigma out of seeking help for mental health struggles." Christine Moutier M.D. Chief Medical Officer, The American Foundation for Suicide Prevention.

# Introduction

• • •

THEY SAY WHAT DOESN'T KILL you, will only make you stronger. After hearing of my suicide attempt Bishop T. D. Jakes asked me "If I gave you a gift, would you throw it away before unwrapping it to see what was on the inside?" Of course I said, "No". He said "Well that's exactly what you tried to do", "You tried to throw away a gift without opening it to see what was on the inside of yourself."

By overcoming my suicide attempt I found that gift. A determination and strength that was buried on the inside of me. By continuing to live to see another day, I have succeeded. This book is my gift unwrapped just for you.

Close your eyes and imagine yourself in a swimming pool, enjoying the hot summer day. All is going fine, when out of nowhere, someone comes from behind and with all of their might pushes your head underwater. You begin to struggle, kicking and splashing water trying your best to knock their hand off so you can take a breath. Fighting and fighting with all you have until you've exhausted all of your energy. You begin to inhale water and lose oxygen by the seconds. The bright sun from that hot summer day now turns into the chilling frozen waters of a winter's dark, moonlit night. Life begins its exit but with just enough energy for one last swing. You knock their hand off! Inhaling life into your lungs like a newborn baby.

One day Satan took me for a little dip in the fiery pool of hell. He strategically convinced me to go for a swim. Once I was in, his grasp became stronger and stronger. He held me under in a coma for eleven hours. We fought, we wrestled, and with one last swing, I was free! Thrusting myself back to the surface for a huge gasp of air…And then I woke up!

This is my story on how depression took control of my mind, persuading me to quit on life. Throw in the towel, as they say. I would have never thought that I would try to commit suicide. Not me! Yes, you!

You remember that time when you lost the best job you ever had and you came home and the eviction notice was on the door. Your spouse left the "Dear John" letter on the mantle. You had no friends to call. School was getting the best of you. Maybe it was as simple as you were just tired of working, exhausted from the daily responsibilities of life, and you uttered the words, "I'm sick of this…life shouldn't be this hard…I wish I weren't even here!" Although you may have only said these things out of anger, repeatedly said they become the building blocks to your suicidal experience.

Prayerfully this book will help you understand how quickly random thoughts of suicide can become your reality. Also this book is for those of you whom made it out to continue living after Satan convinced you to take that little plunge. Hang in there, you are an overcomer. Life is still yours for the taking. Don't give up! There is life after a suicide attempt! Through this book you will see that you don't know what God has in store for you if you would just hold on. You never know what blessings are waiting on you around the corner.

To those of you who have lost a loved one to suicide my heart goes out to you as well. Keep your head up! Although understandably hard, enjoy the great memories they left behind with you! Cherish them, for we all are only visitors here on earth, simply passing through. I honor your loved one by writing this book. Their story is my story. Your family is my family.

# CHAPTER 1

# The Seed of Suicide

• • •

JULY 7, 2003. IT'S MY birthday. "The big thirty." I'm at the tax office, getting my taxes done. What a way to bring your thirtieth birthday in. I know, right! We all know too well how nerve-racking getting your taxes done can be at times. How much do I owe? Am I getting anything back! They say the three things you don't want to mess with are the *I* the *R* and the *S*! So you know my nerves were going berserk!

As I'm sitting in the office, meeting with my CPA, a local newsflash comes over a television set in the corner of the room. The newscaster talks about the death of a teenage girl from an overdose from Tylenol. Drifting away in thought, I thought about what could have been so bad for a teenager to take her own life. Selfishly I thought, *At least she's not having to pay taxes yet, right?* The newscaster went on further to say that it was an accident. She couldn't get over a bad headache, causing her to exceed the dosage amount. Totaling about twelve pills in one evening. It didn't really sound like a lot to me at the time, at least not enough to kill you. Was it an accident, or was it really suicide? Only she and God know. I resumed my meeting with my CPA and finished my taxes, not realizing at the time that only twelve days later, I would be traveling down that same road as the young lady.

In the days that followed, that Seed Of Suicide was planted in my own life. I had been battling with depression for some time now. Unaware on how bad it had gotten, dealing with issues that many of us have faced at some point in our lives. Failed or abusive relationships, investment failures, drugs and alcohol, loss of faith, financial problems, self-pity, character assassins, and the list can go on and on.

I began to focus on all the negative things going on in my life. Magnifying them over and over again until I found myself backed up against the wall. I entered a level of depression I had never been in before. The usage of drugs and alcohol, once a means of having a good time, were now a means of self-medicating and ignoring my struggles and responsibilities. My mind began to play tricks on me, causing me to worry about everything. **Matthew 6:34 says, "Therefore do not be anxious about tomorrow, for tomorrow will be anxious for itself. Let the day's own trouble be sufficient for the day."** Paranoia and anxiety set in, and I couldn't trust anyone around me anymore. Everyone, including friends and family, soon became the enemy out to get me.

The seed was growing faster and faster daily. I was driving down the street one day when all of the sudden, I heard a click and my car began to slow down. I knew I needed an oil change and kept putting it off, and now I had blown the engine! As I got out of the car, the paranoia kicked in again. I felt the eyes of the passing drivers looking at me, watching me get towed off. It was embarrassing to me, and I magnified the situation as if it had never happened to anyone else.

What else could go wrong! Now once again I had to bum rides, which I hated. Leaving me only the option of catching a ride to work, getting dropped off back at home to smoke and drink. Stuck in the house where all I could do was think deeper and harder about all of my problems. *How can I pay all these bills? I can't afford to get my car fixed right now! My business is failing! Should I stay married or get a divorce? No one cares about me! Are they really my friend? I hate living paycheck to paycheck! Week to week! Are my kids better off without me? Who's that looking over here? Is he/she talking about me? Should I go left, or should I go right?* As the Seed of Suicide began to bud!

## THE OIL

*I'm driving down the street*
*My oil light comes on*
*Oh, it'll be all right*
*Another day or two*

*Another night*
*Days go by*
*Again I see the light*
*Ignored it again*
*Now that's not right*
*Just fueling up and going*
*Not taking care of my ride*
*Click Click Click*
*The engine died*
*This symbolized the oil of my life*
**Matthew 25:3 says, The foolish had no oil but the wise did**
**At midnight the Bridegroom came and the foolish had to go buy more oil**
**The wise went into the marriage feast**
**When the foolish came back they said to the Lord let us in**
**He replied I do not know you**
**Therefore watch for you neither know the hour or the day**
*I let my oil run on E and tried to commit suicide*
*Guess I survived on fumes cause I'm still here*
*While in the hospital my family poured oil over my body and prayed*
*The nurse asked me what was the oil for*
*I told her, It represents the presence of the Holy Spirit*
**Psalms 23:5 reads, Yea though I walk through the valley of the shadow of death**
**I will fear no evil for thou art with me thy rod and staff they comfort me**
**You prepare a table before me in the presence of my enemies**
**You anoint my head with oil my cup overflows**
*Now my cup overflows with God's grace and mercy*
*My oil light is no longer on E*
*My oil light of life is on Full*
*My car was stopped*
*But by the grace of God I'm not*
*You have to renew your mind and spirit daily*
*Don't let your oil run out.*

CHAPTER 2

# Game Over

• • •

WITH NO TRANSPORTATION MY BACK was really against the wall. I'd get rides to work, and after work I'd come home and play video games. Work, home, drinking, smoking, and video games. With video games I could leave my reality for the moment and enjoy being a star athlete. You gamers know what I'm talking about. I had the juke and spin moves down, crushing stiff arms, with the ill crossover and fade away, home run hitting to the base stealing, hole in one! Get the point?

Video games have gotten so realistic over the years! They allow you to live the luxury life of buying the best in homes and cars, making large sums of money, all from the comfort of your own couch. Allowing you to reach higher levels after levels, giving you a sense of achievement. Like Drake says, "I just want to be successful," and in recent years, "Started from the bottom now we're here." It was a nice getaway from what I thought at the time of my unsuccessful world.

When I wasn't playing games in the role of the star athlete, I was playing the role of the star idiot. Playing games full of anger, violence, crime, and murder. Running the streets, causing much havoc, hijacking numerous planes, trains, and automobiles. Frequent drug runs and housing large amounts of money. Being a true menace to society. Making Scarface proud. All in the video game land of Grand Theft Auto.

Uncle Sam wants you! With the war going on, it also felt good to play games that allowed me to be a soldier pretending to save America. Back then it was Socom Navy Seals. Now it's Call of Duty and Black Ops. Going on

4

mission after mission, winning badges of honor, rising daily in rank. If only it were that easy. Hostage rescues, ambushes, recon assignments, sniper scopes, riding the land of all terrorism, capturing Bin Laden or Sadam Hussein. At the time the majority of all my game playing was spent on these more violent types of games. I thought in some kind of way that these games relieved more of my stress. They soon turned out to only intensify it. The loud surround sounds of music, fast cars, roaring fans, AK-47 gunshots, explosions, mixed with the alcohol and drugs, only fueled my anxiety and paranoia even more. I was in a spiritual war and had no idea.

By no means do I blame my suicide attempt on video games. I'll just say that the viewing of repeated acts of violence, and the roller-coaster ride of success and defeat, wouldn't have been what the doctored ordered for my present state of mind. I still play video games today from time to time, just not as much. The addiction to video games can be very dangerous in some cases. Just remember, the reality of life begins when the game is over.

## SLEEP ON THE EDGE OF THE BED/EGGS OVER EASY

Along with the games came an abundance of sleeping. I would stay up all night, playing video games, dreading going to work in the morning. At times I would just be plain lazy and call into work and sleep, drink, smoke, and play games all day. I didn't have the passion for my job anymore, and my business was definitely paying for it. **Proverbs 24:33 says, "A little sleep, a little slumber, a little folding of the hands to rest, and poverty will come on you like a bandit, and scarcity like an armed man."** We all know we need sleep to perform properly, but too much of anything isn't good for you, not even sleep. **Proverbs 20:23 says, "Diverse weights are an abomination to the Lord."** I had no balance at this point, and without balance you're surely to fall.

I once heard a preacher quote the nursery rhyme story of Humpty Dumpty. I never heard this one on the pulpit before. It was hilarious when I first started hearing him talk about it in that old-time Baptist preacher voice, whooping and hollering, but it turned out pretty interesting. I'll break it down for you how I got it. You've heard the story before!

*Humpty Dumpty sat on the wall*
*Humpty Dumpty had a great fall*
*All the King's horses and all the King's men*
*Couldn't put Humpty back together again*

OK, here you have an oval object, an egg, attempting to sit on a flat surface. No balance! It's destined to tip or roll over. The combination of unrighteous living and the lack of time spent seeking the Lord will never balance on God's scales. **Matthew 6:33 says, "Seek first his kingdom and his righteousness and all things shall be yours as well."** You should make a habit to seek God first throughout each day. This is the true beginning of balance.

The preacher went further and talked about the wall that Humpty sat upon. The foundation! What have you been sitting on? What's been your foundation? In an old Christian hymn titled "My Hope Is Built on Nothing Less" written by Edward Mote, the songwriter says, "On Christ the solid rock I stand/All other ground is sinking sand." Boy, was I sinking! How about you? Is your life built on the solid rock or on the sinking sand? In **Matthew 7:24** Jesus gives the parable of the wise and foolish builders. It says, **"Therefore everyone who hears these words of mine and puts them into practice is like a wise man who has built his house on the rock. The rain came down, the streams rose, and the winds blew and beat against that house; yet it did not fall, because it had its foundation on the rock. But everyone who hears these words of mine and does not put them to practice is like a foolish man who built his house on the sand. The rain came down, the streams rose, and the winds blew and beat against that house, and it fell; and great was the fall of it."**

Just like a home, you need a solid foundation to begin. Be wise and stand on the word of God! For in the time of trouble when the winds begin to blow, and the trials of life rise and beat against you, you'll know how to handle them. You may get knocked down, but because your foundation was built on Jesus, you know that you can get back up! Remember "On Christ the solid rock I stand/All other ground is sinking sand."

The nursery rhyme doesn't tell you how high the wall was. It just states that it was a great fall, just like the foolish builders. Therefore, you don't have to be on the mountaintop to fall hard. You can be stumbling in the valley, and it will hurt as well. Meaning from the president to the homeless person, no one is exempt from the great falls of life. Look at all the high-profile people who also hit rock bottom! We all are vulnerable, and one wrong step away from having that great fall.

That's why it's important to stay humble. Success often brings forth a bit of pride. **Isaiah 2:11 says, "The haughty looks of man shall be brought low, and the pride of man shall be humbled; and the Lord alone will be exalted in that day."** No one really knew how stressed and depressed I was, not even myself. Many people thought I had it all together. They would say things like, "I wanna be like you when I grow up," or, "If I had your hands, I'd cut mine off." Behind closed doors I knew the truth, and so do you. Like Public Enemy said, "Don't believe the hype! Don't let the world's perception of you send you to hell! Thinking you all that!" That's where the scripture **Mark 8:36** comes into to play. **"What profits a man to gain the whole world and lose his own soul?"** Worry about how the Lord sees you! Is the Lord pleased with your works? Being on a pedestal or in the spotlight can be nice at times, but it can also be the set up for your great fall. Be careful up there! Am I preaching to somebody?

The preacher then said turn to your neighbor and say get up, Humpty! If you do fall, it's OK. Get back up. After you fall don't look for man to put you back together again. The rhyme said all the king's horses and all the king's men couldn't put Humpty back together again. Isn't it nice to know that we don't need the king's horses or his men? We can get help directly from the King! How great is that!

Another songwriter Tramaine Hawkins writes in the classic Gospel song "The Potter's House", "You don't have to stay in the shape that you're in/The potter wants to put you back together again." Sometimes in times of despair, we seek for relief in man, but just as in the nursery rhyme when they couldn't find comfort for Humpty, neither can man find comfort for you. Therefore, seek the king!

Learn to forgive yourself your mistakes and then move forward! **Psalms 32 says, "Blessed is he whose transgression is forgiven, whose sin is covered."** The blood of Jesus has already washed your sins clean. Accept your forgiveness! Donnie Mcklurkin's song says it best. "We fall down, but we get up." Brush yourself off, get back up, and try life again! Seek God's instruction first before seeking advice from family and friends.

Now check this out! OK, now I want you to compare yourself to a raw egg. It's shell is very smooth yet fragile. The protection is there, but it's very weak. With the slightest blow, the damage is done. Once cracked its insides begin to pour out, just like you and me. Whether it's a nasty rumor or a fierce right hook. As they say your face is cracked. Your shell is weak, the tears or blood soon follow, and your insides begin to pour out, just like a raw egg.

When the raw egg has been boiled, it becomes tough. The shell is no longer smooth; it's rough and bumpy. It's not as easy to get to its insides. You can drop it and nothing comes out. You can crack it, but now you have to peel its skin. That weak, fragile shell becomes strong with layers of protection. So just as the boiled egg, once you have been tried in the fire, once you've gone through some trials in your life, you, too, become stronger. In **2 Corinthians 12**, Paul pleads to Jesus to take away the torments of the world that affected his flesh.

**Jesus replies, "My grace is sufficient for you, for my power is made perfect in weakness."**

**Paul replies, "That is why for Christ's sake, I delight in weaknesses, in insults, in hardships, in persecutions, in difficulties. For when I am weak, then I am strong."**

In other words, don't let the smooth skin fool ya! You may feel weak, but know that you are strong! After the fire...the trials, the things that use to bother you don't bother you the same way they used to. Yeah, you might still get your face cracked, and that right hook might still hurt, but your skin is a lot tougher now. You've learned how to handle things better. You've developed some coping skills. And guess what? After being boiled and then peeled, that oval egg can now sit up right on that flat surface. It has balance! That's something, huh! I know I'm a genius for that one, right! Lol!

When you get through the protection of that boiled egg, now you're humble and on your way! A little salt and pepper and it's all…mmm mmm good! **Matthew 11:28 says, "Come to me, all who labor and are heavy laden, and I will give you rest. Take my yoke upon you and learn from me; for I am gentle and humble in heart, and you will find rest for your souls. For my yoke is easy and my burden light."** It may take some time, some labor, a little work to get there, but once in, you'll find rest and enjoy the meal. Transfer your yoke for God's yoke. I never knew how important the story of Humpty Dumpty could be! I bet you'll never sing that nursery rhyme the same!

My own bed had become so uncomfortable for me. Restless nights soon followed, pushing me closer and closer to the edge of the bed. With one careless rollover, I began my descent to the greatest fall of my life. Just like Humpty.

CHAPTER 3

# Boiling Point

• • •

JULY 18, 2003, DEPRESSION AND fear took over me. My mind had become very fragile and sensitive. Mere jokes became real threats, and mere gossip became the truth. I took everything close to heart and had lost trust and faith in everyone I thought I could believe in. Friends, family, God, and worst of all myself. Who were these so-called friends of mine that I was hanging around from time to time? Were they really people I could trust? Did they have my best interest at heart? I didn't know anymore! It's a real scary feeling to wake up one day and feel like you can't trust anyone, not even family! You have no true friends! It was all fake, a mirage, and you're a loner!

I couldn't sleep that night! I spent the whole night awake! I didn't know what was going on with me. I was feeling a way I had never felt before! I was hot! I felt backed into a corner and didn't know who or what was coming to get me. My mind began to spin out of control! Normal loud sounds like cars driving and honking down the street or the ringing of the telephone began to scare me! It was like a was living out the song "My Mind Is Playing Tricks On Me" by the Geto Boys.

*"At night I can't sleep I toss and turn... Four walls just staring at me... I'm paranoid sleeping with my finger on the trigger... I'm popping in the clip when the wind blows... Every twenty seconds got me peeping out my window.*

*Day by day it's more impossible to cope... Can't keep a steady hand because I'm nervous... Every Sunday morning I'm in service... Praying for forgiveness... I know the Lord is looking at me... But yet and still it's hard for me to feel happy...*

*I often drift when I drive… Having fatal thoughts of suicide… Bang and get it over with… And then I'm worry free but that's bullshit."*

All lyrics from Scarface, one of the group members, who in more recent years has admitted to dealing with mental illness and depression in his life.

Not aware of it, I began to say good-bye to some friends and family. I knew I was bugging out, but I had a couple of people I could still trust, at least I thought. I also recalled dropping my daughter off at daycare earlier that day, and her looking over her mother's shoulder waving good-bye as though she knew it was her last time seeing me. Oddly enough I found some comfort in knowing that she was safe away from my confusion. Something strange was definitely going down, and as long as my kids were fine, I was OK with whatever it was! I was completely losing my mind. I was no longer myself.

The heat was on, and the war was just beginning. Instead of arming myself with the word of God, I armed myself with my grandfather's old shotgun and hunting knife! I spent the whole night pacing the floors and looking out the windows. Sorta felt like I was Malcom X in that famous picture, armed and ready, protecting his family, looking out of the window. **Ephesians 6:11–12 says, "Put on the full armor of God so that you can take your stand against the Devil's schemes. For our struggle is not against flesh and blood, but against the rulers, against the authorities, against the powers of this dark world and against the spiritual forces of evil in the heavenly realms."** The gun or knife couldn't help me with what I was up against! I needed the helmet of salvation to protect my head and to protect my mind.

By sunrise July 19, my mother had gotten word of my condition. She came over my house to see about me. I let her know how much I appreciated her for doing the best she could have done as a single mom raising a son. Letting her know how much of a great job she did. I was saying good-bye, and she was picking up on the signs. She knew then I was giving up on myself, and she wouldn't let me out of her sight.

It was a Saturday morning, and I was supposed to be at work. I wanted to just sit and be alone, but my mom got me out of the house and made me go to work. By trade I am a cosmetologist and barber, so she knew I had clients scheduled for a Saturday morning. She stayed at work with me the whole time, trying to snap me out of whatever was going on with me. By this time I was completely out of my mind. It was as though that I was having an out of body experience. I was talking to myself, not verbally but to my conscience, if you will, building up different scenarios in my head. *Who is my mom on the phone with? Why is this client here today? That ringtone on my mom's cell phone is driving me crazy! I can hear my heartbeat in my ears. It sounds like a rushing wind is all around me! My head is pounding!*

After work I wanted her to take me back to my house so I could be alone. She wouldn't leave my side and instead took me back to her house to spend the rest of the evening with her.

Once there she told me to take two prescription sleeping pills that she had from a previous prescription and to lie down and go to sleep. I told her no and continued to pace the floors from one room to the next, mind racing. While walking the halls of my mother's home, the Seed of Suicide began to blossom! My mother had been taking care of my grandmother and step-grandfather who were elderly and both living with her. He had passed away about a year prior. The Lord took him in his sleep in their room at my mother's house. As I paced the halls from room to room, I entered my grandparents' bedroom and thought about him. He was such a great man. A deacon in the church for many years and a true servant of the Lord. *I would love to go like he did,* I began to think. Just to fall asleep and wake up with God. That was the way to go! No pain, no stress, just go to bed for the night and rise in the morning with the Lord. Tis so sweet! Well done, thy good and faithful servant. A fitting reward for a man such as him.

While I was sitting on the same bed that took him home to glory, I was being mentally tricked into taking my own life. "You can go to sleep like that, too," the Spirit of Suicide spoke.

Sitting there, confused, I noticed a bottled of Tylenol PM on the nightstand next to the bed. I picked up the bottled and never looked back. The deception that I could sleep my pain away sat in, and I did not take into consideration that I may not arise with the Lord as my grandfather had. Most people believe that if you commit suicide, you'll go to hell. I'll let you be the judge on that one. Who really knows? Weren't we taught that Jesus died for all of our sins? He took all sin to the cross, right? One sin is no greater than the other, right? Did Jesus have to die? Didn't he give his life? If you really look at it, in my opinion, Jesus was sent on a suicide mission, by himself. So did Jesus commit suicide? Just a thought.

"Your mother said she wanted you to go to sleep," the Spirit of Suicide said.

Taking the bottle into the kitchen and getting a glass of water, I began to swallow pill after pill, handful after handful, until the whole bottle was consumed. I was totally out of my mind at this point and all rational was gone. The Spirit of Suicide had completely taken over me. I then went back to my mother's room and told her that I would go ahead and take the two prescription pills she offered me earlier and lie down. She gave them to me, and I took them as well. I couldn't go to sleep, still pacing the floors. I went back to my mom and told her that the pills weren't working and could I have a couple more. She told me to just lie down. They were very strong and would kick in soon. I was fully engulfed with the idea of sleeping my life away. I needed the anxiety, and paranoia to go away.

Up the hall, down the hall, over and over again, I paced. I entered the kitchen where I found a cabinet full of pills. I was so caught up in what I was doing I wasn't even thinking anymore, totally wrapped up in another realm. Any many miny mo! I grabbed another bottle of pills, and without out any voice of reason, I began on my second bottle.

When I was halfway through the second bottle, the doorbell rang. I went to the door and noticed that my vision was blurring. It was hard to see through the peephole. The pills were taking their toll. Since I couldn't see who was at the door, my paranoia wouldn't let me open it, so I walked away.

With half a bottle of pills still in hand, I could hear my mom at the door talking to someone. "Hey, Dave." I heard a deep calming voice, causing me to hide the remaining pills behind some books on the bookshelf in my mom's office. It was my cousin, who I called my uncle. A man of the cloth, a preacher I hadn't seen in years. We called him *uncle* because he made you feel like you were one of his own kids and not just a cousin. That one person that you could always call on when things got a little too hard to bear. He truly had the light of God shining through him and on all who were in his presence! "Hey, Dave!" When I heard Uncle Red's voice, it was though God had walked right up into my mother's house and was like, "Boy, what are you doing?" I felt like a child in trouble with his hand caught in the cookie jar, but in this case it was the medicine cabinet!

"Come on in here and talk to me and tell me what's going on," he said.

We went into the back of the house to be alone and talk. With me sitting on the couch and him sitting in a chair right in front of me, I remember telling him that I felt like a failure and had let my family down. I was ashamed of the many bad decisions I had made along the way, and I was just tired of myself. He began to encourage me and pray for me. Then only about twenty-five to thirty minutes after me taking the first pill, while talking to Uncle Red, I finally went to sleep…Into a coma! My mother would have to tell you what happened next!

## MOMMA'S BOY (A PARENT'S ACCOUNT), WRITTEN BY CHERYL PAXTON, MY MOTHER

Let me go back a little bit in the story so I can tell you how my morning began that day. The phone rang, and I looked at the clock, and was 7:20 a.m. on a Saturday. It was David's wife, and I could tell she was upset.

I said, "What did he do now?"

They had been separated for some time now and were going through some rough times at this point in the marriage.

She responded, "Mom, I think he's talking about killing himself!"

I said, "What?"

She had been with him for a while the night before but had just left him to go check on their kids. Panicking I got out of bed and threw something over my gown and rushed over to his house as fast as I could. Racing to the front door, I knocked. With no answer I began banging! *Am I too late?* I began to think until I saw him peeking out the window. He came to the door, and he had this evil-looking smirk on his face.

With his eyes glazed like he was looking right through me, he said, "Momma, what you doing here so early?"

I walked in the house and told him, "Well, your wife is concerned about you." I sat down, and he walked to his bedroom.

He came back to the living room and asked me again, "Momma, what you doing here?"

"Well, I hear you're wanting to hurt yourself!"

He wouldn't sit still. He was a nervous wreck, and again he paced back into his room and then back into the living room, and again he said, "Momma, what you doing here?" Almost like he didn't believe anything I was saying. Then he said, "I know, I know, you're trying to save your baby boy like always."

It was as though I wasn't even talking to David at this point. If felt like a demonic spirit had taken over him. He sat down next to me and stroked his hand down one side of my face, then got right back up and went to his room. He came back with his Bible, turned to a scripture, and began to read a verse. I don't remember what verse it was, but after reading it, he said, "See, Momma, I haven't lead that type of life."

I said, "Well, son, we all have fallen short in this walk. Jesus has already paid that price."

That evil spirit just smiled back at me with that smirk on its face again.

I looked at the clock and said, "Shouldn't you be getting ready for work? I know you have clients. It is a Saturday morning." I knew I needed to get him out of the house and keep my eye on him.

We went to his shop, and he did my hair and then worked on a couple clients. While he was working, I was on the phone, making calls to his father who lived in DC to inform him what was going on. I also called his sister, who was on the road going out of town at the time. We all began working together to figure out what to do as a family. His sister called their cousin, Red, who was a minister to come talk to him, and his father began looking for flights to book to bring him to DC, so he could get away and relax for a while.

When David finished working, he asked me to drop him off back at his house, but I told him, "No, not while you're talking about hurting yourself."

He kept saying he was fine, trying to convince me, but I took him over to my house anyway, so I could keep him safe. Once home I told him to lay down and get some rest, but he just kept pacing up and down the hallway. I went to my room to pray and lay down myself, for it had already been an exhausting morning and afternoon, and I did not know that this was only the beginning. The evening would soon turn into a nightmare. While I was lying in my bed, David walked in and sat on the edge of the bed and started rubbing my back.

He said, "Momma, are you going to be OK?"

I replied, "No, not until you are OK."

Then he looked at me and said, "Momma, you have given me every opportunity to be the best I can be." Then he began to rub my back again, asking, "Momma, are you going to be OK?"

When I think back on it, he was trying to assure me that his actions were not my fault. I knew he had not been asleep much at all for the past four days, so I told him to take two Elavil pills I had and to go to sleep, but he said no and walked out of the room. I could hear him walking up and down the hallway, still pacing and going in and out of my mother's room, but I didn't know what he was up doing. I wasn't really concerned with him hurting himself because I figured as long as he was in the house and there with me, he was fine. I simply just wanted him to go to sleep, and soon I got my wish.

Eventually he came back into my room and asked for the pills, so I gave them to him, not knowing that the plot was thickening. I'd say about twenty minutes later, he came back in my room and said, "Mom, these pills aren't working. Can I have some more?"

I told him it would kick in if he would just settle down and relax and get some rest. By this time the doorbell rang, so I came out my room to answer the door, and it was their cousin Red. I told David that someone was here to see him. When David came out of my office, he had a strange look on his face, like the cat that had swallowed the canary. I did not even know he had more than the two Elavil pills. David and Red went into the den to talk.

About thirty minutes later, Red came back into the house and said, "Well, I must have talked him to sleep. I couldn't keep him awake."

So in my mind, the Elavil was working, so that was a good thing for me. Red said to have David call him when he woke up, and he left. I walked into the den, and David was sitting on the couch asleep. I started walking back into the living room when my spirit spoke to me for me to wake him up and tell him to go get in the bed so he could get some good sleep.

I went back into the den and said, "David, get up and come get in the bed," but he didn't respond, so I walked out again.

But my spirit just would not leave me alone. All I kept hearing was, *Wake him up.*

So I again I went to den, and very loudly I shouted, "David, come on!"

And he didn't budge at all. I physically started trying to wake him up, pulling him up by his arm. At first I thought he was just playing around, and jokingly I said, "OK, I'm going to call 9-1-1," again no response. While pulling his arms up, I grabbed his hands, and that's when I saw a prescription bottle top fall in slow motion out of his hand and begin rolling on the floor! It felt like a ton of bricks falling and hitting my stomach, knocking the wind out of me. I screamed, "Boy, what did you do!" Panicking I began yelling, "Get up, David! Get up!" All I could think of was what you see on TV when this kind of thing happened, shaking, slapping, and splashing them with cold water, trying to get them to walk around. I was running around like a chicken with his head cut off! I didn't know what to do. I wet a towel and put it on his face.

I was in such a panic and state of shock, but then out of nowhere, a peace came over me and said, "Stop acting like a mother and remember you are a nurse." I made sure his airway was open while calling 9-1-1. I told the dispatcher what was going on and that I was indeed a nurse, and she told me help was on the way. I kept checking his pulse and talking to him, telling him to hold on. Faintly I began to hear the sirens from a distance coming into the neighborhood, and as the noise grew louder and louder, I ran and opened the garage door. The fire department, police department, and EMSA were there. They rushed in and took over!

"What did he take?" they asked.

I told them I didn't know. All I gave him were two Elavils. (Of course in hindsight, I realized you should never give someone prescription meds that aren't prescribed to them.) The police went through the house, looking in all the trash cans for empty bottles so the paramedics could figure out what David had taken but found nothing. The paramedics checked his vitals, picked him up, strapped him to the gurney, and rushed him into the ambulance. Everything happened so fast. He was transported to Saint Anthony's hospital. I got in my car to head over, and it was the longest drive of my life. It was like I was in a dream and everything was happening in slow motion. I was in a daze.

When I walked into the ER, I heard a nurse shout, "I don't know what he took, but it's more than two Elavils in his stomach." She had just finished pumping his stomach. When the report came back, it stated it was also Tylenol and traces of weed.

I thought to myself, *Well, there was a bottle of Tylenol in the cabinet, but it only had two or three pills in it.* I just assumed he had a reaction to the Elavil.

At this point the doctors and nurses had done all they could do for him. Now it was a waiting game. There I sat and watched my baby lie in a coma. Several hours had passed, and he was still not waking up. He was strapped to the bed in pose restraints and four-point restraints because he was very combative. We watched him buck, struggle, and fight for over ten hours straight. It was hard to watch. We all sat around his bed, crying and praying the whole time.

I remember at one point just laying my head on his bed with my eyes closed, and the Lord began to show me what was going on in the spirit. I could see my baby at the gates of hell, trying to get away, and then I saw a hand from above reach out to him, and David caught hold of the hand, and right at that moment he abruptly woke up.

He opened his eyes and he said, "Momma, change of heart."

I didn't know what that really meant at the time. I was just so thankful to God that he was alive. I asked him, "Son, where did you get the Tylenol?"

And he said, "Grandma's room."

Then I remembered I had just bought her a new bottle of Tylenol PM, and it had been sitting on her nightstand in her room.

He was then transported to the ICU so they could continue to monitor him and to infuse the antidote for the Tylenol. He wasn't talking much. He was still so confused. He would look and stare around the room in a daze. It was as though he wasn't himself. I didn't see the eyes of my child. I would look him in the eyes and say to him, "I love you, David, and God does, too."

A couple days had passed, and word had gotten out what had happened to him, and people were flooding the hospital. The nurses began to ask, "Who is this guy?"

With all the visitors coming by, he became very anxious, so the nurses shut down his visitation. It was past visitation hours, but I wasn't leaving my baby. I told them I apologized for being there past hours. The nurses were very nice to me and said it was OK and that I was what he needed.

When the nurse left, he moved over and notioned me to come over and get in the bed with him. It was so cute. He whispered, "Momma, don't tell nobody I had you get in the bed with me."

I laughed and said, "OK, son."

He laid his head on my chest and slowly began to fall back to sleep. I was watching the monitors, and his heart rate slowly went down from 118 to 80 instantly. That was a surprise to me, even as a nurse.

The next day his antidote was completed, and it was time to asses his mental condition. By this time his father had made it into town, and we transported David to another hospital with a lockdown unit. We got there, and they explained to us what would occur while David was there in their care. That first day leaving him there was the hardest. I remember when we walked out of the unit and the doors locked behind us. David was standing there looking through this small window, and he had such a confused look on his face. Like, "Momma, why are you leaving me here?" When the elevator doors shut, I started crying. I got home, walked in the house, and it hit me. My baby just tried to take himself out of this world. I fell to my knees and collapsed, stretched out on the floor, and cried my eyes out. I was exhausted. It had been a very rough four days.

This book is dedicated to my mother Cheryl Paxton. What mother can say she gave life to one child two times? Thank you for always being there when I need you the most. I love you.

# ENTERING HELL

*You see some of us think of hell as a place where you go when you die if you're bad*
*Or a place we tell kids they'll go if they're bad.*
*And that you can get to it by grabbing a shovel digging deeper and deeper*
*You know where the Devil lives*
*With the pitchfork and everything*
*We need to shatter that description of hell*
*God cast Satan to the earth*
*The very place you and I live*
*Stop telling your kids that the Devil lives underground*
*Tell them the truth*
*Hell is among us all*
**I Peter 5:8 reads: Be sober, be watchful. Your adversary the Devil prowls around the earth like a roaring lion seeking someone to devour.**
*When you were born you physically entered hell*
*The older you get, spiritually you chose how you live in it*
*Your choices will determine how you live here*
*If you choose not to follow the commandments of God, the deeper you get into hell*

*Stop digging*
*The Lord doesn't want you to live this way, but he will not force you to serve him*
*God gives us free will to choose how we will live on earth*
*Just as Adam and Eve had a choice in the garden, you have a choice as well*
*Heaven or hell*
*When you live in righteousness, you can maneuver through Hell like God's very own secret undercover agent*
*You can see the Devil coming a mile away*
*When you live in unrighteousness, you become the Devil's prey*
*We all are here physically*
*But spiritually we are living in two worlds*
*Ask yourself, are you experiencing heaven on earth or are you living in hell*
*Hell is a place where you are totally separated from God*
*Where you will forever thirst after God's grace, not water*

*When the Bible talks about how hot hell is and the fire in hell*
*It's making reference to how terrible and painful it will be not to have God's mercy*
*How your soul burns to be with the Lord*
*Some of us have been burning in the fire of hell so long that we don't even feel it anymore*
*Conformed to the world*
*Conformed to living in hell*
*We think of hell as an afterlife experience*
*Instead of realizing that, depending on how you are living your life,*
*You may be experiencing hell right now or at least the beginning stages of it*
*No telling what's coming next*
*If you were to die right now*
*Would you want your soul to eternally be separated from God?*
*When you were born, you entered hell*
*Don't die in it!*

CHAPTER 4

# Date Night

• • •

ONE OF THE QUESTIONS PEOPLE asked me most when I got out of the hospital was, "Do you remember anything while you were in the coma?" This was a very sensitive question for me at first because some of the things I couldn't really tell if I was awake or not for some of the things I recall because it was so real to me. Also I wasn't sure how people would respond to some of the things that I claim I saw and heard. I had to realize, whether or not they believed me, it was truly what happened, and that's all that mattered! I don't know why. I can't explain why! The timing of the things my mind reflected on during this time is still amazing to me. Im not sure if I can explain it on paper! It was like a dream, but it wasn't, or was it! It was as if episodes of my life were being played on the big screen, and I was at the movies, eating popcorn, watching from my hospital bed.

Sounds of music echoed my mind as if I had earphones on. A melody played over and over in my head. It sounded familiar, but I couldn't recall the words of the song or the artist at the time, only the instrumental. It was like my suicide soundtrack or something! For whatever reason it wouldn't go away! *Is someone playing this song outside my room? Am I awake? Am I dreaming? What's going on! Where is that music coming from?*

When I got of the hospital, I could still hear the melody to the song playing over and over in my head. I knew I had it at home somewhere. I hummed it and hummed it until I figured it out! Turned out it was "Who Do You Believe In" by Tupac Shakur. I pulled it out and played it over and over as I reflected on the day I actually met TuPac.

It was the summer of '94. I was walking down the street with some friends in Time Square in New York City. The streets were very crowded with people everywhere. It was my first time in New York, and all the lights and busy streets of Time Square amazed me. I had never seen anything like it. It was fast, raw, and grimy! With XXX signage everywhere! It was everything I'd seen in movies. All of the sudden, in the midst of the crowd, a guy walked by right next to me.

One of my friends said, "Hey, man, that was Tupac."

"Yeah right," I said. And kept walking.

"Naw, man, that was Pac," he repeated.

Still walking I began to think to myself, *What if it really was Pac? When will you ever get a chance to meet Tupac?* As a matter of fact, I was returning to Oklahoma City the next day. I turned around with just enough time to catch a glimpse of his bandana tied around his bald head before it disappeared into the crowd. I had to see if it was really him!

So we started to run through the busy streets of Time Square to catch up to him, but we had lost him, so I stopped. I scanned the crowd but couldn't find him at first. When all of a sudden, there he was! I could see him through a glass window of a local record store, with his head down, looking through some old albums! Wow! It was really him, and he was all alone! I went into the store and walked right up to him and said, "What's up, Pac!"

He said, "What's happening?" We dapped up! Shook hands for y'all that don't know what that means.

I must admit I was a majorly star struck. I mean this was Pac! "Brenda's Got a Baby"! "When my Homies Call"! "Dear Momma"! "I Get Around"! Keep Ya Head Up"! Come on, man, I was "juiced!" Some of y'all might get that, LOL! I told him I was a big fan, and I didn't really want much, but if it was cool, could I take a snapshot with him? He said it was all good. We took a couple of shots, and right about this time, a group of girls that was with me and my homeboy finally caught up with us. They came in the store and bum-rushed him! They took over, trying to hug and kiss on him, it was funny! He was real cool though and took pictures with them as well. We shook hands again, and we all walked out of the store together. While leaving the store, a peddler came up to him, trying to sell him one of those hats with the multicolor paneled umbrellas on the top of it. It was funny at first. Tupac told the guy, no, he was fine. The peddler walked up behind him to try to make his sale again, and that's when it got serious!

Tupac turned around this time with his hand behind his back in the stance like he was clutching a gun and shouted at the guy, "I said I'm OK."

Our laughs were immediately silenced. In his defense I understood because he was by himself, no security guard at all. We stood there in shock as we watched him disappear into the crowd. Not even knowing only two years later he would be killed.

Of all the songs that could have played in my head at this time! Why this one? "Who Do You Believe In." What was God trying to say to me! Through one of the most controversial rappers of all time. Tupac was someone that battled with multiple personalities, depression, anxiety, and paranoia. He even battled with suicidal thoughts. He makes reference to all of that in his music. "Now I'm lost and I'm weary, so many tears/I'm suicidal, so don't stand near me," a verse from the song "So Many Tears" released in 1995. He was a poet, and there are even some who believe he was a prophet! He said it best: only God could judge him. It's not my or your job to determine where his soul lies. All I knew was in some odd and strange way, God used this song to get a message to me.

The debate is whether or not Tupac is still alive. Whether he is or not, I know his spirit still lived through his music on that day to try to encourage me. His spirit will continue to live on in the heart of many friends, family, and fans. I believe that if he was still alive or if his spirit was trying to get a message through to his friends and family today, it would be the same message he got through to me. Asking us all, "Tell me, who do you believe in?/I put my faith in God blessed and still breathing/Even though it's hard that's who I believe in/Before I'm leaving I'm asking the grieving/Who do you believe in?"

Me with Tupac in Times Square in 1994

Another remembrance I had were the voices of some people saying poetry. For the past couple of years, every week I had been hosting an open mic poetry night that was making a deep impact on my community. Lives were being changed, and chains were being broken. I'd seen the most reserved people evolve into local stars! As for me myself, I never considered myself a poet. I just offered the venue and played the music. Only after my suicidal experience did I begin to write.

Listening to the pages and pages of the good and the bad times of life that each one of them had experienced encouraged us all. There was the Black Pride

Poet, giving everybody the lowdown on slavery, segregation, and the plot of the man. The Political Poet speaking out on social issues and history as it referred to the African American and its relevancy to the present. The Erotic Poet, who's lustful and enticing words would have the women checking for moisture and the men adjusting their pants. The Gospel Poet inspiring us all with words of correction, soulful healing, spiritual knowledge, hope, and wisdom.

There were words of hurt, abuse, rape, drugs, joys, pains, and laughter. Not a topic untouched. Nas came out with a song "All I Need Is One Mic." It was as though that was what the people needed in my community. One mic, so their views could be heard. An outlet to release deep-down, bottled-up pain that had tormented them for years.

Here was an opportunity for everyone to be heard. No discrimination of color, sex, beliefs, or lifestyles. It was your platform for the moment to get whatever off your chest! The mic also gave some people the chance to display other art forms as well, like paintings, African drumming, comedy, dancing, rapping, and singing.

Our poetry night brought out unknown musicians, radio personalities, inspiring producers, club owners, and promoters. Talent filled my little shop, the Hair Café, Barber Shop, & Salon! Soon the adult atmosphere of spoken word, aromatherapy, the very best in soulful music, wine, and hors d'oeuvres created a new nightlife for the city.

Why it had even been said that poetry night at the Hair Café was the Mecca of poetry for Oklahoma City! If you hadn't done poetry here, then you hadn't gone through your poetry rights of passage as a poet in Oklahoma City! I didn't say it, another poet did! A true compliment and a testament on how groundbreaking this night was to the city. Not that it was the first poetry night ever, I'm sure, but it was the first poetry night to have the impact it did. Launching open mic poetry nights to the next level in our city.

As the era of Russel Simmon's Def Poetry Jam ushered in, it only grew bigger and bigger, causing a poetry wildfire in the community. Poetry nights were popping up all over the city now. The art form was growing rapidly week to week! In some ways it was good and in some ways bad. It kind of watered the market. Everyone wanted a piece of the poetry pie, causing a lack of consistency because it spread everyone out. Our market wasn't big enough yet to handle that. Two or three poetry nights a week in different locations was too much. Plus certain nights didn't deliver the same atmosphere that ours did, putting a bad taste in the mouth to the newcomer of a poetry night. But I was just proud of what we had accomplished and happy to see the art form grow beyond our walls.

Poetry nights at the Hair Café were taken very seriously. Our host, Grace, made sure of that! The Lyricist Lounge embodied a certain energy no other night could achieve. We had no idea that so many people were hiding all that talent to themselves. Whether the crowd was nine or ninety-nine the poetry went on. With some of the more poorly attended nights turning out to be the most radical, inspiring, and energetic nights of all. If you missed them, you missed them. Your loss!

We realized that it took a lot for a person to get up in front of a crowd of unknown people and spill their guts out. It took a lot of confidence that plenty of us are lacking. This was a way to build or regain that confidence you once had until it was taken away by some mishap of life. So respect of the poet or entertainer was a must! First timers to our mic were given a standing ovation upon taking the stage. No talking! Give them your attention! Snap, clap, cheer, give them the respect they deserve for performing for you! In some other venues, it turned into a "who's there" event, a party atmosphere, or only about making money. It wasn't about the art. We truly did it for the love of it.

While in my coma—I think! LOL—I recall being in the atmosphere of poetry night. I could hear music and the voices of familiar poets as if they were there, telling me to hold on and be strong, just relax, it's just another poetry night. We're here with you! Thanks to you all! Y'all my people! I know y'all were there with me! I could hear y'all, I swear. Snap! Snap!

Earlier in the year, I had gone to a church program called *The Autopsy of Jesus*. It was based on a very thorough examination of a doctor performing an autopsy of Jesus after the Crucifixion. The torment his body went through, and the torture he endured. A very detailed description of all the weapons of torture used and the damage each one of them would have to the human body. The program had very graphic sounds of torture, pain, and agony. To say the least, it was somewhat scary! R-rated would be more like it.

Every blow, every cut, and every drop of blood was accounted for. There was also an explanation on how to perform a perfect and proper crucifixion.

The measurements and weight of the cross. The exact size and placements of the nails and even how to stretch the arms out of the sockets for proper placements! They stretched him wide and hung him high. It gives me chills thinking about it as I write this. This play was horrific but at the same time it was very interesting to really understand the torture that Jesus went through.

While in the ICU, in my coma, I can remember hearing the same sounds of torture, pain, and agony. My mind immediately went to the play at church. All the moaning and groaning that I heard were all the exact same sounds I was now hearing. The exact same sounds! It was as if the sound engineer from the play was in the ICU, playing the same sound bits from the play. At the time I thought someone was. As a matter of fact I was certain someone was.

Could all these sounds just be coming from other patients in the ICU? Maybe. Or was I at the gates of hell, hearing all the torture, pain, and agony one would face upon entrance? My mom told me later that I bucked and bucked back and forth while I was in the coma, like I was fighting and wrestling someone. Either way. Why was my mind reflecting on that play, *The Autopsy of Jesus*?

I believe it was God's way of reminding me that he had already paid the cost for everything wrong I had done. Why was I trying to pay for my wrongs with my own life? He had already gone through the torture, pain, and agony just for me! Every bone-crushing blow, every vein-bursting cut, was all for me and you! Your sins have already been paid for.

So to some it all up, while I was in my coma, God played me some Tupac. We hung out at Poetry Night. And God reminded me that he died for me, my sins were forgiven, and I was still his. It was my Date Night with God. And guess what. He wants to date you, too!

## I NEVER THOUGHT I'D WRITE A POEM LIKE THIS

*I never thought I'd write a poem like this*
*Sitting here holding this bottle of Tylenol*
*Wanting to end it all*
*All aboard! This train's headed straight to hell!*
*One pill!*

*Two pills!*
*I downed the whole bottle!*
*I'm out!*
*Wait a minute!*
*Is that music I hear?*
*Someone's whispering poetry in my ear!*
*Grace, is that you or you Soul Secure?*
*Let me off! Let me off!*
*This is a train I could've missed!*
*I never thought I'd write a poem like this!*

*I never thought I'd write a poem like this!*
*Out for eleven hours*
*Let's see what all did I miss*
*That ride to the hospital, It had to be crazy*
*Police, Ambulance, Sirens just a blazing*
*I can't recall a gag or a choke*
*They pumped my stomach*
*Now charcoal down the throat*

*MRI scan, well, let's check his liver*
*His liver's OK. ICU was the next place delivered!*

*Doc told my family*
*Well, that's all we can do*
*Hope he wakes up or he'll*
*Be done too!*

*Man...I don't remember none of that shit*
*And still ain't figured out how they got that catheter in my dick!*

*I never thought I'd write a poem like this*
*Hell, I didn't start writing*
*Till I was in the psych. unit!*

*So y'all just gone leave me here*
*My family waved bye*
*While wiping away the tears!*

*The door was locked*
*My view was through the window*
*As their elevator doors closed real slow*
*Check out your new home*
*Down the halls I began to roam*
*How long would I be here?*
*The answer unknown*
*Damn! My name's on the door*
*Like its been waiting all my life*
*Come on in, the door cried*
*Come on in for the night*

*A bed for me to rest*
*Better than a grave*
*Can't be scared to lay in it*
*This is the bed that I made*
*Two weeks past*
*Made it through this big ordeal*
*Within those two weeks*
*I have so many stories to tell!*

*See I defeated suicide like Jesus defeated death!*
*And I'll keep praising his name till I breathe my last breath!*

*So now as I bring this sermon now to a close!*
*I never thought I'd write a poem like this*
*But who knows!*

*It could have been you!*
*It could have been you!*
*It could have been you!*

*But just remember*
*That he rose!*
*That he rose!*
*That he rose!*

*And you can see him again and again and again!*

*Depending on the path*
*You have chose!*
*You have chose!*
*You have chose!*

*Yeah, he's coming back*

*That's the train that you don't wanna miss*
*I never thought I'd write a poem like this!*

## How

*They say to get where you're going, you must know where you been*
*So sit back, relax, here's where the poetry began*
*Mother's Day at the tender age of nine*
*Wrote Moms a poem 'bout beatin' my behind*
*And it read:*
*Mom, even though you kick my butt*
*And you give me uppercuts*
*I still love you anyway*
*So Have a Happy Mother's Day! ( Snap! Snap! Snap!)*
*On to the sixth grade*

*Thanksgiving Poetry Contest*
*Picture in the* Black Chronicle
*To the students poem that was best!*
*Well, well, well, what more can I say*
*Gobble! Gobble! Gobble!*
*As I gloated that day!*
*Time passes on*
*Never recognizing my gift*
*My pen and my pad was on the shelf*
*And there it remained to sit*
*And sit it did just the same as I*
*But The nightlife was dead*
*We Needed something new*
*And now was the time*
*The idea came*
*Open Mic Poetry Night*
*Live at the Hair Café*
*The Lyricist Lounge would be dubbed the name*
*Met with IIndigo and Grace*
*To Discuss time date and place*
*First night twenty-five*
*Second night forty-five*
*Till it got so packed*
*You wouldn't want to be late!*
*We guaranteed you your five minutes of fame*
*No longer to be unheard or unknown*
*'Cause now we all know your name!*
*All eyes on you aprroaching the mic with ease*
*Watch out you might turn into an overnight celebrity*
*Def Poetry Jam soon followed and it was a huge hit*
*Russel Simmons definitely put his stamp on it*
*Next thing you know*
*Everyone wants a piece of the poetry pie*

*I got a lil' ticked off I ain't gonna lie*
*But who am I, the owner of poetry?*
*That's what it's all about, your words being free*
*Free to be expressed wherever you choose*
*Whether you receive cheers or you receive boos*
*So here we are today…*
*Now the scene has been up and, yeah, it's been down*
*But the poetry scene still lives, just look around*
*Again they say*
*To get where you going, you must know where you been*
*It's plain and simple*
*It's time to hear from you, my friend*
*I've told you how we started*
*To get where we're going, here's what we must do*
*Your words to live*
*Discover the poet in you*
*The Mic is yours*
*Your talents feel free to display*
*You're always welcome here*
*At the Hair Café!*

*Poetry contest winners shown in* The Black Chronicle Newspaper, *1984*

CHAPTER 5

# I'm Still Here

•  •  •

IT LOOKS SO BRIGHT! REMINDS me of the movie *Poltergeist*. When the mom says, "Run to the light, Carol Ann!" It felt like I was in a dark tunnel, and I could see the light coming from the other side. I was on my way up, out from that fiery pool of hell!

I recall seeing the face of my uncle, the last person I'd seen before diving in. I began to swing at his face, trying my best to reach out to him, causing me to start stroking like a swimmer. Swimming faster and faster, thrusting myself back to the surface! And immediately, as if I had been holding my breath underwater the whole eleven hours, I rose up off the bed like a dead man out of a coffin. And with a huge gasp of air, I was free. After reading the segment my mother wrote in Chapter 3, I got chills. When she said God showed her what was happening in the spirit, it totally lines up with what was going on. It was my uncle Red I was reaching out to, and if you recall in the beginning of my story, I said that when I heard his voice when he came to talk to me, it was as if God had walked right into my mother's home. I reached out for Uncle Red while reaching out to God at the same time.

When I opened my eyes, the first thing I saw was the cross hanging on the wall above my hospital door. The room was so bright that immediately I had to close my eyes. The reflection from the light blinded my vision, but I could still see the cross. Only now it was a cross full of colors floating around the room. You know the effect you would get from staring at the sun or a light-bulb too long and then closing your eyes. In the old Christian hymn titled "At The Cross" Johnny Cash writes, "At the cross at the cross where I first saw the light and the burdens of my life rolled away. It was there by faith I received my sight and now I am happy all the day." The cross just bounced around the room from wall to wall in a rainbow of colors. A sign telling me to keep my eyes on the cross, and on Jesus! He was in control!

Wow! Was I awake or was I asleep? Reality set in as I noticed that I was strapped to the bed in full restraints.

"Are you OK, David?" my mother said. "You must have been in a real spiritual fight, son. You've been jerking, bucking, and fighting the whole time." "She said at one point I rose up and said, "Momma, change of heart," and went right back down and continued fighting". I told her I was fine.

I was still looking for my uncle Red. "Where is he?" I asked. "I just seen him." They told me that he had been there to pray but had been gone for some time. I could have sworn that he was there! Guess the good Lord used him to save me from the beginning to the end. Reaching out for my uncle Red pulled me out from under.

A nurse walked in the room and asked me, "Do you know what happened? Do you remember what you did?"

With a trembling voice I told her yes. I felt so guilty and ashamed at that point. Although looking back on it now, I never wanted to die. I just wanted my mind to stop racing. I needed the confusion to end.

Not knowing what was to come next, I became even more frightened. The thought of facing the world now felt more stressful than before. All the questions they would ask, the comments they would make. I didn't want to face that either.

Believe it or not, the Spirit of Suicide was still busy! Maybe you can take this oxygen tube and wrap it around your neck and hang from the bed and just finish the job off. Or maybe you can get up and run and jump out of the window. The thought of facing the criticism now was making things even worse than before. The anxiety and paranoia were even more magnified now.

Right about that time, I needed to use the restroom. "What the hell is this?" I said as I began to pull this strange tube coming out of my, well, you know, my private area. The nurse rushed back in and told me that I would be very sorry if I tried to pull it out! It was a catheter. The embarrassment of knowing that people I didn't know saw me naked was a very weird feeling to say the least. She carefully took it out and unstrapped my arms from the bed. I got up and went to the bathroom. So, I'm sitting there, thinking about everything, you know where you do some of your best thinking, the toilet. I couldn't believe all that had happened in so little time. I reflected on things I remembered before the pills, during the coma, and now the aftermath. It was a lot to take in.

After a while I got up and looked in the toilet, and to my surprise my bowel movement was *black*! I mean tar black! Jet black! It freaked me out! I thought I had messed up my insides for good! I came out in a panic!

"What's wrong with me? What's going on?" I shouted.

The nurse had to calm me down. She told me that it was black from all the charcoal that they had to pour down my mouth when they pumped my stomach. An experience that I'm glad that I was not awake for. I don't remember any of that. I was told that when you get your stomach pumped, it's not a very friendly situation. It can be very painful and hard on your throat. The charcoal was used to soak up all the poison I had taken. All I could think was, *What have you done!* Now I really knew where the saying came from because I truly felt like a black piece of shit.

The next few days were a complete blur. I lost track of all time and the days of the week. I had no idea how long I had been in ICU. Later I found out that I was there for about three days.

Some months prior to my suicide attempt, I had gone to a gospel concert featuring an artist by the name of Dorinda Clark-Cole. A member of the famous gospel group the Clark Sisters. The concert was packed! One part of her show was dedicated to a suicidal experience she had gone through. She testified that one day she was fed up and was going to drive her car off a bridge into a river!

Dorinda testified on how calling on the name of the Lord saved her life, causing her to turn around and go home. At the concert that night, she began to sing a song titled "I'm Still Here," a song that she wrote after going through her suicidal state. It's a very powerful song! If any of you readers have had the honor of hearing this song or especially having heard her sing it live, you can testify to how powerful and anointed this song really is.

Anyway, the song had everyone standing up shouting and crying. While singing it she walked, shouted, and danced around, sharing her testimony and giving out as many red roses to guest that she could. I wondered what the roses were for. Have you heard the saying "Give me my flowers while I can still smell them?" I suppose that was what she was doing. Giving everyone she could a rose to smell life, for them to realize that they were still here in the land of the living! No matter what you've gone through, at least you're still here!

Standing in the back of the room, watching in amazement, I saw Dorinda walk over to my mother and reach out and give her a rose. Out of all the hundreds of people that were there, my mother was one of the few that received a rose that night. Dorinda had no clue how the Lord was using her in my family's life. It was as if Dorinda were encouraging my mother to be strong for what she was about to encounter. To hang in there, it was gonna get rough, but this too would pass! I watched in astonishment how powerful her testimony was and the effect it was having on the body of Christ, not knowing soon we would share the same experience.

Even though I had lost faith, my family kept me lifted up! They knew that repentance and prayer were the first stop on my road of recovery. They brought me a Bible and a CD player. My sister put in a CD, and the first song that played was Dorinda's "I'm Still Here"! What was crazy was that, because I still wasn't fully in my right mind yet, I couldn't even remember where I had ever heard it before.

That song became my battle cry! I put it on repeat and played it all day and all night! And I do mean all day and all night, no exaggeration. Twenty-four for three days straight. No one was to touch it! Noone was to stop it! Noone was to change it! I was drawing so much strength from it! As I listened to the words of the song, I began to realize that God saved me from death and had a reason for me to still be alive.

I realized that I was in a war, and boy, was I being attacked! The Devil almost achieved checkmate, like we were playing chess, but God gave me one last move. Prayer! I remember asking my mom to get in the bed with me, and I laid my head on her chest like a new born baby, listening to that song all night! Picture that a grown man in the bed with his mom! In a little hospital bed! Go ahead and laugh. I'm laughing, too! Hey drastic times cause for drastic measures!

She was the only one I thought I could trust! What do I say after all of this, Momma? How can I be forgiven from this? I didn't know what to say to God. She told me that if I didn't know what to pray about, then to just say Jesus! **Philippians 2:10 says, "That at the name of Jesus every knee should bow, in heaven and on earth and under earth, and every tongue confess that Jesus Christ is Lord to the glory of God the Father."**

**James 2:19 says, "Even the demons believe and shudder."** Still weak from all the trauma I inflicted on my body, I closed my eyes and began to simply say, "Jesus, Jesus, Jesus," over and over again. I was on my way to recovery!

When the disciples asked Jesus to teach them how to pray, he said pray then like this. **Matthew 6:9: "Our Father who art in heaven, Hallowed be thy name. Thy kingdom come, Thy will be done on earth as it is in heaven. Give us this day our daily bread; And forgive us our debts, As we also have forgiven our debtors; And lead us not into temptation, But deliver us from evil."**

The Lord's Prayer, a prayer that I've come to realize we as people today don't take as seriously anymore. Sometimes when we do things over and over, we don't seem to care about them as much anymore. They just becomes habit. I believe most people just say the Lord's Prayer in repetition, and it's just a routine prayer for them to say.

From sporting events, to school programs, to the dinner table. Come on, let's say the Lord's Prayer before the game so nobody gets hurt. Say it so we can eat! Aw, that's so sweet. My child knows the Lord's Prayer.

Those are all fine, but keep in mind what a serious and powerful act you are engaged in. Think about it. Jesus taught the disciples how to pray with this prayer! That's powerful within itself! You're giving reverence to the Lord, asking him to keep you in his will! You're asking him for all that you need to make it through the day, your daily bread! You're repenting and asking for forgiveness, with the realization of knowing that you will only be forgiven according to the level of forgiveness you've given others! You're asking him to keep you from the things that cause you to sin! Keeping you from all evil till his kingdom come! Amen!

Understanding the power in this prayer is a key essential part of your spiritual growth and the basis of your prayer life, just as it was to the disciples. I understand the Lord's Prayer in a whole new light now, and I pray that you do as well.

I started reading the Bible that my family brought to me. The Lord led me to the story of Daniel and how God delivered him from the lion's den. The Bible says that Daniel was a man with an excellent spirit. He had a lot of jealous men conspire against him because of the high office he held. They wanted to find some kind of fault in him. Sounds like politics and the hierarchy of social society we live in today. Right?

When they couldn't find fault in him, they made up a new law, stating that no man could pray or give reverence to no other god or man than King Darius for thirty days. Daniel continued to fall on his knees three times a day to pray and give thanks before his God. When the men found that out, they went to the king and told him that now they had found fault in Daniel, for he was not following the law. They convinced the king to stay true to the new law, and for this wrong Daniel should be cast into the lion's den. The king commanded Daniel to the lion's den and said to Daniel, "May your God, whom you continually serve, deliver you!"

The king was troubled all night, and the Bible says that sleep fled from him. At the break of day, the king hurried to the den and with a troubled cry, said, "Oh, Daniel, servant of the living God, has your God whom you continually serve, been able to deliver you from the lions?"

Daniel replied, "Oh, King, live forever! My God sent his angels and shut the lions' mouths, and they have not hurt me because I was found blameless before him and before you!"

Then the king ordered Daniel out of the lions' den, and ordered that all the accusers of Daniel, their wives, and children be placed in the lions' den! The Bible says that before they could reach the bottom of the den, they were overtaken and their bones were broken into pieces. In other words they got ate up!

There is a lot to learn in this story, for the Daniels in the world today and you accusers out there also. Let's start with the accusers. **Romans 13:13–14 says, "Let us conduct ourselves becomingly as in the day, not in debauchery and licentiousness, not in quarreling and jealousy. But put on the Lord Jesus Christ, and make no provision for the flesh to gratify desires." Romans 14:1–4 says, "As for the man who's weak in faith, welcome him, but not for disputes over opinions. One believes he may eat anything, while the weak man only eats vegetables. Let not him who eats despise him who abstains, and let not him who abstains pass judgment on him who eats: for God has welcomed him. Who are you to pass judgment on the servant of another? It is before his own master that he stands or falls. And he will be upheld, for the Master is able to make him stand."**

God places people into positions that he sees fit. Its not up to us to challenge that decision. You may even think that a person's past doesn't qualify that person to receive God's blessings. Why him or her, Lord? I don't like him or her! I remember when this or that! Sure, you might think that someone else or even you are more qualified for the position, but be patient and let God work on your behalf. Your promotion may be right around the corner.

Who are you to pass judgment? Don't go out developing schemes, trying to satisfy your fleshly desires to put that person down. The Bible teaches that if God is for you, who can be against you. It's very dangerous to go against God's appointed, anointed, or chosen. It cost the accusers of Daniel their lives. Not only that, their whole lineage was killed! So be careful when you go out trying to destroy someone else's life, because you may be setting yourself and your whole family up for destruction.

For the Daniels. The one thing that stuck out to me in this passage is that when the king cried out to see if Daniel was still alive. He replied, "My God sent his angels and shut the mouths of the lions because I was found blameless before the Lord." Sometimes we can be our worst accuser. We look back on our past and come to the conclusion that we are not worthy of God's blessings or certain positions God places us in.

Sure, we've done some wrong. There are some things that you are to blame for, but through Jesus you are forgiven. You can't change your past. Forgive yourself, repent, and move on! **Ephesians 1:7 says. "In Jesus Christ we have redemption through his blood, the forgiveness of our trespasses, according to the riches of his grace, which he lavished upon us."** You're forgiven! Stop blaming yourself! You, too, yes, you, have been found blameless before the Lord!

It said that God sent the angels to shut the mouths of the lions. Another famous scripture comes to mind, **Psalms 23:4–5, "Even though I walk through the valley of the shadow of death, I fear no evil; for thou art with me; thy rod and thy staff, comfort me. Thou preparest a table before me in the presence of my enemies."**

What do we do at the table? We eat! The lions represent your guest—the enemy sometimes being yourself, the "inner" you. Daniel represents the feast (you). The den represents the table (your situation). Wherever God has placed you is your table. Whatever arena that is: work, home, marriage, church, sports, politics, illnesses, school, etc. The stage is set. The table is prepared for all to dine with and in some cases on you. You will have plenty of guests to sit at your table throughout your lifetime. Some will be friends, enjoying your presence, and others will be wolves in sheep's clothing, lions preparing to feast on you.

Here's what you do. What is the one thing we always do before we eat? We pray. Whenever it feels like the main course is being served and you're on the menu, and the lions begin to open their mouths, when those accusers begin to speak—he or she is no good! I should be in charge! I can play football better than him, my jump shot is better, I should be the pastor, the president, I would have made a better husband or wife, etc.—do as Daniel and continually serve God! Begin to pray! Thank God for the criticism, opposition, and trials. Praise God as he leads you through the valley of death! He will shut the mouths of the lie-ons (lions).

# CHAPTER 6

# Break Out the China

● ● ●

A NEW TABLE WAS SET for me. Suicide! I was thrust onto a new stage for all to see. Soon the hospital was flooded with many visitors. Some of them in from out of state. *How did they get here so quickly?* I wondered as I lay in my bed. My bed faced a glass wall allowing me to see each visitor as they walked up the hallway and made their way to my room.

I wondered what were they thinking and when they got in town. I tried to play it cool as each of them entered, asking how I was doing. "Aw, I'm all right! What y'all been up to?" The things we say when we're in denial about how we're dealing with the many different situations we go through in life. I'm sure I looked pretty crazy, saying that I was cool with oxygen tubes coming out of my nose. That's funny!

Each new face that suddenly appeared from around the corner of the hospital hallway, coming to my room brought forth so many different emotions. When you're in the hospital and people who don't really visit you when you're doing fine come to visit, it is a weird feeling. As I lay there, it was like being dead in a casket, looking through dead eyes, watching each person make their way closer to me. Like if they were in line at a funeral for the final viewing, walking down the aisle to view the body and shake hands with the family.

Just imagine watching your own funeral. Who would show up? Family, friends, enemies (lion's). Why did that person come? Why didn't he or she come? It was a very confusing and overwhelming time for me, but for whatever reason each visitor came I saw that I had an impact on a lot of people. I truly thank everyone who reached out to me during this time. It gave me strength to keeping pressing on.

As the news spread, more and more people came. Causing my mental state to go haywire again, as the blood pressure cup continued to drive me crazy every other minute, blowing up and down on my arm. Like they say pressure burst pipes, and I was past that point. I felt so boxed in. Face after face, emotion after emotion, until it was too much for me to handle. I became angry and violent, and couldn't understand why all these people were coming to see me. I was told that so many people called and showed up that the hospital shut down all my visitation. I was too paranoid for that many visitors. I felt like everyone was out to get me and had their own motives for being there, including family. I just couldn't wrap my mind around the fact that they were all just truly concerned.

Three days had past, and they figured it was time to get me out of there. I was grateful to all of those who came to visit me, but all I wanted to do was disappear, crawl away in a hole, and be left alone. My mom handed me a business card that read, "The Best Way to Make Your Dreams Come True Is to Wake Up." I just kept saying I wanna disappear. My mom would just smile and laugh and say well just wake up.

"Are you ready?" she kept asking me. "Just wake up, son!" Now of course I was physically awake, but she was talking about a spiritual awakening.

"Are you ready?" Again my family continued to ask.

So since I just wanted to get out of there, I was just like yeah. I had no idea what was about to happen next. My head was still so cloudy, kinda like the feeling of a severe sinus headache with an extreme amount of pressure, causing me to constantly pat and hold my head.

*Am I going home? What's happening?* I remember a nurse coming in saying something like, "They have room for him over there." I didn't know what was going on. Everything was happening very fast. Next thing I knew, they were taking off the blood pressure cup. The nurse was wheeling in a wheelchair. My family was saying, "We're right behind you," and they began to sweep me off into the sunset. So at least I thought!

I sat down in the wheelchair, and down a back hallway, I began my trip to an unknown location! As the thought of Tupac and the pictures of him when he was being wheeled out of the hospital after his failed murder attempt came to mind again. I was in an extreme state of paranoia. Where was I going? Where were they taking me? I had no clue.

Going down on the elevator, I recall looking at the numbers of the floors as each passed by. Five, four, whose gonna see me when these doors open? Three, two, feeling like the paparazzi would be there taking pictures! One, *ding*! The doors opened, and no one was there, thank God!

Down the hall I could see doors leading to the outside. Closer and closer the nurse wheeled me. My family was no longer with me. I began to look for them in panic as we exited the hospital. I was dazed and paranoid, and the thought of being outside for the first time was very uncomfortable. The sun was so bright outside as I sat in my wheelchair, waiting for my family, thinking they were pulling the car around. I looked at the many cars in the parking lot, wondering who was looking at me. I just wanted to be alone so bad. If I could have gone to the moon, I would have, but unfortunately my spaceship came in the form of a shuttle bus. "The little bus!" *Am I on the crazy bus?* I thought.

The nurse wheeled me on with a couple of other people and told me to take care. I was really bugging out now! Where the hell was my family! I was quiet the whole time, as the bus drove down the street. Looking out of the windows, I couldn't recall any of my surroundings. Absolutely nothing looked familiar to me. I didn't know if I was on the north side, east side, west or south! Would you get in a car with strangers not knowing your destination? I don't think so! So imagine how freaked out I was, it was as though now I was being kidnapped! I was scared!

I was just riding along, not knowing what my fate was. I felt somewhat tricked by my family! My head felt like it was about to explode! It felt like I was being shipped off to jail or something. Little did I know that I was indeed about to be locked up!

## THE SOLOIST

After about fifteen to twenty minutes after leaving the hospital, we pulled up to another unrecognizable building for me. They let me off and wheeled me into another hospital! Now I was back on another elevator, only this time it wasn't going down. It was going up. Again the floor numbers began to stand out. One! This was getting real crucial! Where was my family? They said they would be right here! Two...three...and *ding*!

I was wheeled up to a set of double doors, and the nurse buzzed an intercom and announced my name, and the doors opened! I was wheeled in, and the doors were locked shut behind me! *This can't really be happening to me,* was all I could think. I began to pace the floors up and down the hallways, passing a host of unfamiliar faces. Patients of all races, young and old.

I recall stopping to look out of a window, trying to figure out where I was, but still no luck. I had no clue. Out of the window, all I saw were cars speeding one after another. Red light, green light. The cars were moving so fast they were a complete blur, causing my nerves to go in a frenzy again. I began to hold my head as a phone began to ring loudly, snapping me back to reality. David! Someone shouts my name, telling me that the phone was for me. On the other end, an aunt of mine that I hadn't spoken to in years. She tried to comfort me, telling me that my family would be there soon. I began to shed a few tears. I was so scared.

A nurse walked by telling me to calm down and keep my composure. I started looking around the room at the many people that we all would describe as crazy. Yelling, screaming, and laughing to themselves. My first thought was to head for the door and try to escape. About the same time of that thought, two very large security guards walked through the doors, fully equipped with guns on there sides.

*Wow! I'm really locked up! I'm in the crazy house!* Upon this newfound reality, my family walked in.

"You OK?" they asked.

"I guess so," was my response. They began to hug and comfort me before they were lead into a private room to speak to a counselor.

Still dressed in my hospital gown, scrub pants, and footies—what a site, huh! LOL!—I continued to walk and pace the halls. From the nurse headquarters to the lounge to the dining hall. Patients, nurses, orderlies, security guards, so many faces. I questioned myself. *Do they know me? Who is that? Why are they looking at me?* I was so paranoid and terrified.

My family approached me, finished with their meeting, a meeting that turned out to be my admission to the unit. They told me to be strong, get some rest, and to hold on and that they would come see me in the morning. We all hugged, and I walked with them to the dreaded double doors and waved bye to them through the windows as the doors slowly closed. Watching them leave in disbelief as they entered the elevator, and them looking back at me in just as much despair while their elevator doors closed. And then they were gone.

## THE SOLOIST

*I was off to see the new movie* The Soloist, *starring Jamie Foxx. After purchasing the tickets, I proceeded to the theater. Before entering I noticed that the Department of Mental Health had a booth at the entrance. They were passing out information about mental health issues.*

*It caught me by surprise because I really didn't know what the movie was about. I simply thought it was about some guy who was a good musician and ended up homeless. Someone found him and helped up get off the streets. He would then make it back to the top and be one of the greatest musicians ever. Boy, was I wrong.*

*It all hit me during the movie when Jamie Foxx's character began to fold under the pressure. The success and the high level of expected performance he found while attending music school soon wore on him. The whispering voices of inadequacies and doubt began to bounce around in his head. The voices caused a chain reaction of paranoia and anxiety. He reached out to his family for help because he knew something wasn't right anymore. But just like most of us do, they ignored the warning signs of his mental state and didn't get help. They simply said, "Oh, you'll be OK." Basically suck it up. Sometimes there was a little more to it than that, as they soon found out.*

*As he began to play his instrument among his peers, the fear of not being good enough overwhelmed him. "They can hear you. You're not good enough." The whispering voices spoke to him, causing him to play out of tune. As the voices bounced around in his mind and through the surround sound speakers of the movie theater, I remembered the voices coming from the left and whispers from the right, echoing failure after failure in my own life.*

*It took me back to when I did the same thing. It made me remember the paranoia and anxiety and how it took me over. It was really a hard movie for me to watch, but I didn't want the people I was with to know I was tripping out. Everything from the whispering voices he struggled with to being part of mental health group sessions brought back many thoughts. It was so real I wanted to get up and leave because it brought back so many memories of my fight, but I fought through it.*

*Jamie Foxx did an excellent job with his portrayal of this character. I believe he should have gotten a Oscar for this role. You would have to be a person that has gone through that type of turmoil to really understand how well he played it. Thank you, Jamie Foxx, for taking on such a challenging role that dealt with a very strong issue that most people, especially African Americans, don't like to talk about.*

*Fact is we all have to become "The Soloist." In our own lives, we have the abilities to play the instrument and gift of life every day! You are an instrument! How well you play it is totally up to you. Sure it takes practice. Yes, you will face criticism and rejection from others. Just keep playing, and fine tuning yourself through all adversity and obstacles. Even if you have to stand alone, find your sound, find "The Soloist" in you!*

*Never knew the impact Jamie Fox would have on me when
I got a chance to meet him back in the '90s*

CHAPTER 7

# Who's Your Daddy?

• • •

I REALIZED THAT I WAS indeed alone, locked up, and wasn't going anywhere. My first night began in the lounge, sitting on the couch, watching television. Staying to myself, I didn't want to talk to anyone while observing the different patients walking around.

"I want my daddy" a lady began to mumble. "I want my daddy," she screamed this time.

*Is she mocking me?* I thought because that was exactly what I was feeling at the time, and I'm sure I looked like a lost kid wanting his parents.

"I'm a write my daddy a letter," she yells. With a very strong country accent, again she screamed, "I'm a write my daddy a letter."

She walked over to the nurses' station, and they gave her a pencil and a piece of paper. The lady then came over to the couch where I was sitting and sat right next to me. When I say that she sat right next to me, let me rephrase that. I meant to say as she began to sit down, her butt ran down my shoulder, down my arm, until she was basically sitting right on my hip, shoulder to shoulder. Words can't describe the thoughts that were going through my mind. All I could think was, *Is this lady sane enough to be around other people with a sharp item like a pencil?* What if she just bugged out and started poking people? Let's just say I jumped up and got the hell away from her.

"Dear daddy," she screamed as she begins to scribble on the paper. None of it was legible. "Dear daddy." Again talking to herself, when all of a sudden she jumps up, grabs her pen and paper, runs down the halls screaming and waving her sheet of paper. "I'm a write my daddy a letter. I'm a write my daddy a letter!" With both hands, I began to hold my head again! It was then that I realized that I was indeed in for a very long night!

Hearing her talk about her dad did in fact make me think about mine. We didn't have the best of relationships while I was growing up, but boy, was I glad to see him during this most traumatic time in my life. Growing up without a father in the home is something that I'm sure a lot of you that are reading this book can relate to, male or female. It's a topic that I myself had never gone to any psychiatrist for, but I'll just give you some of my views and thoughts on the subject from a male child's point of view.

My parents divorced when I was very young. My father was a military man in the navy, so with us living in Oklahoma, we never lived in the same state. He did his best to keep in touch from time to time. I knew who he was but didn't really know who he was as a person. I always wanted him in my life, though.

Like most kids in single-parent homes, when the parent they are living with would discipline them, I would say I wanted to go live with my daddy. I felt like my mother couldn't understand where I was coming from as a young man growing up because she was a woman. Over the years I visited and lived with him here and there, but that father and son relationship never matured as we both would have liked.

From time to time growing up, I would hear other kids talk about their fathers. I would hear them say things like, "My dad always said that you should do this when…Or when this happens, you should do that." It always sounded really cool to me to hear them say stuff like that. I really envied them for having their fathers around to give them some instruction. Sometimes I would sit off to myself and try to think what I would say if I were the kid saying my dad always said you should do a certain thing in a particular situation. I always wanted to have that one thing to stick my chest out about and say my dad said you should…

Although my pops did help out financially, which is indeed a blessing in itself, that father and son bond was still needed. The visual affection, correction, and the love of a father is just as important as the caring and compassionate love that a mother displays. They both have their places in the home. One cannot survive without the other.

When the father is absent in the home, it causes the mother to play the role of compassionate care giver and also the role of the hard-core ruler and enforcer. Causing a unhealthy imbalance of affection in the home. Leaving the child without a resting place or shoulder to lean on in times of correction. In some cases causing the child to find that resting place in places outside the home. Finding refuge in such things as smoking, alcohol, drugs, sex, and even gang activity. Which leads to underage smoking and drinking, teenage drug addiction, countless acts of premarital sex and abortions, and the life of crime, jail, and unfortunately premature death that usually occurs with kids involved with gang activity. The child is forced to find personal validation and acceptance from the streets instead of in their own home.

A child often seeing the proud smiling faces of their father can motivate them to great heights. In some cases the lack of seeing those smiles also finds its place in the motivation of a child wanting to show their father what he missed out on. Either way it leads me to believe that the encouragement of a father is very important in a child's development.

Who can tell you that your jump shot is looking real good better than your own father? Or that if you keep playing like this, we'll be seeing you on Monday Night Football or in the Major Leagues. All encouraging words from a father that became the driving force for many athletes in professional sports today. Those encouraging words are more so provided by mothers today.

How about the male bonding between father and son as the father teases his son as he catches him checking out a girl for the first time. Or the bonding of father and daughter as he teaches her how to be a lady and how to be treated as such. Both helping to form the early developmental stages of their sexuality that will carry on from their adolescent years into their adulthood.

Helping a child develop self-confidence is important as well. Teaching a child how to stand tall, proud, speak up for themselves is very key. Instructing them on how to handle peer pressure, bullies, and many other intricate plots of the Devil that they will encounter in the school systems today is vital to their development. This confidence can be achieved by not only the father but also the mothers expressions of affection and appreciation to the child. Also with rewards of verbal praise when the child does well in specific areas. These are things that will help the child find that personal acceptance and validation in the home instead of at school or in the streets.

By the time a child reaches their teenage years, some distinct characteristics have been set in them. How they behave, choice of friends, music they like, clothes they choose to wear, foods they like to eat, self-discipline, learning skills, acceptance to authority, etc. These choices could last a lifetime for a child. When those choices are disrupted by a parent that comes in a child's life at a later period, it can cause the child to rebel.

The child feels like he has been forced to develop his life on his own, and how could that be challenged by anyone that wasn't there from the beginning? I call that the back-end parent. A parent that tries to instill their values, beliefs, rules, or goals on their child after the child is no longer a child.

There's a saying, that you have to see a man to be a man. The father has certain roles around the house that children need to see. Not only things like taking out the trash, or cutting the grass, upkeep on the car, or paying bills. Leading his family to the Lord is his number one duty. **Proverbs 22:6 says, "Train up a child in the way he should go, and when he is old, he will not part from it."** Training a child how to seek and find comfort in the Lord is the most vital thing a parent can teach a child. Teaching them the importance of prayer and repentance. Showing the child that the way to go is to commit themselves to the Lord. That way throughout their life when things get a little heavy and the trails of life seem to become to much for them to bear they know how to call on the name of the Lord. A child seeing his father's commitment to the Lord and his family is the first symbol of commitment they should learn. Thus showing them how to commit to the Lord, a marriage, their schoolwork, extracurricular activities, jobs, or even the commitment of paying bills.

Growing up I felt incomplete by not having my father around. I couldn't understand how you could leave a child to just wing it as they say. Man, it's rough out here in this world! With the many trails and issues that everyone faces on the earth, how could you leave it up to a child to just figure it out! I can remember saying things like, "When I get married, I'm not ever getting a divorce."

Although there was a lack of fatherhood in my home, my mom played both roles great. She also encouraged me to develop a relationship with the Lord. I learned to receive instruction from my heavenly father. She inspired me to pursue and develop a prayer life with God. It was through that relationship of prayer that I began to start praying for my father's salvation on a daily basis. I begin to ask the Lord to just watch over my father and to touch him in a way that would inspire him to begin to seek God. I didn't really know if he had a relationship with God, but even as a child, I knew that prayer could change that if he didn't.

Over the years God began to work on the relationship between my father and me. Whereas before there was a lack of communication, my father began to call more. I began to see God moving in his life, and I knew for myself he was seeking instruction from God for direction in his life. Days of fatherless instruction soon faded away. Even as a man well off in my thirties now, by having that fatherly instruction, I began to feel good in knowing that I could gain insight for the day-to-day challenges I faced today as a man.

Forgiveness fell in my heart for my father. I could no longer hold the bitterness that had built up in me over the years for not having him around. Now I thank God for that "back-end parent," and the time that we still have together. I realize that having him around now in my adult years as a man have proven to be very beneficial to the both of us. In some cases having him around now has proven to be just as beneficial, if not more than having him around in my younger years. Im so grateful and thankful for that. So I had to let those younger years of frustration go.

Now myself a father, children out of wedlock, a child living out of state, and also having gone through a divorce, I see now how difficult and trying it can be to be that perfect picture of a father. It's funny how life can brings things into perspective for you. The things you said you would never go through find a way to creep up on you to see how you would handle them yourself.

Now I talk to my father about how to deal with the emotions of having a child out of state, or how to handle the emotional trials of going through a divorce and being separated from your children. Before as a child, I only thought about how the separation affected me. Now I see for myself how the separation affects the father as well. I knew my dad loved me even though he wasn't around, but now I see for myself how difficult it was for him.

I thank God my dad and I have developed a better relationship. It's been great for not only me but for my children as well. He's a wonderful grandfather, and if my suicide attempt would have succeeded, I would have never seen our healing take place. Forgiveness was the key. God forgives you in the same measure you forgive. I would advise any child dealing with the issue of not having your dad around to somehow in your heart forgive him. It's not too late to develop that relationship. As long as the two of you are still here breathing, you all have a chance. Of course every situation is different, and I know that some things may be a lot harder to let go of. I get it. I'm just saying it's never too late to give it a shot. You have to let go of the past and move forward. It can prove to be beneficial for the both of you and your generations to come. It's not just about you anymore.

I did finally get that one thing to stick my chest out about that my father instructing me to do. Along with a host of plenty more, but this one is something that I've personally grown to appreciate more over the years than I think I would have as a child. My father instructed me to the book of Proverbs, a book of instructional poetry. He taught me to read the chapter that corresponded with the current day's date, and when the month ran out, to start all over. Now this might sound little to you, but it really inspired me to get into my word. And to this day when I get sidetracked and off focus, I turn to Proverbs to put some things back in perspective.

There is so much instruction for the many challenges that we all face in the world today found in the book of Proverbs. As you begin to read each chapter daily, you realize how to implement these instructions into your everyday life. By taking heed to these instructions and uplifting messages, you can avoid the many snares of the enemy that are set for you. I have found myself in many of those snares time and time again, but thank God for his grace and mercy to get it right today. The reason this one instruction by my Father stands out to me more than anything else he has instructed me on in my adulthood is because I know my prayers were answered. Those many nights of being a young child saying my prayers at night, asking for God to keep my dad covered and prick his heart, leading him to God. It had really happened. And I'm still here to see it with my own eyes. He goes to church now. He prays with us now. I can see God's wisdom on his life. I'm proud to be his son.

Now not only to the fatherless child but also to whomever reading this book needing guidance in their life. I would say first and foremost know that you have a heavenly father that loves you more than you can imagine. I understand if your situation does not permit you and your earthly father to get things straight. Just know that you can always go to your heavenly father; he's only a prayer away, and he'll be a father like no other.

Secondly I would like to invite you to the book of Proverbs as my father instructed me. I've begun to pass this instruction on to my kids' friends and family also. You take it and invite your loved ones to it as well. As it is passed around daily, it will touch the lives that need to be touched to break the cycles that need to be broken to make this world a better place to live in.

Third, I would like to say, I love you, Dad! Thanks for being there when I needed you the most! I look forward to the many years to come! You're the best!

My father Charles David Threatt and I, at the Oklahoma City
Out of the Darkness Walk for Suicide Prevention in 2014

Whew! Got that out, now back to the story. After reflecting on my dad, it was time for bed. The nurses made everyone go to their rooms. I headed to mine. Up unto this point, I hadn't been to my room yet, but when I made it, I noticed that my name was typed on a piece of paper taped to the door. There was also another name typed on the paper as well. To my surprise there was already someone asleep in my room. I had a roommate.

The thought of going to sleep in a room with someone I didn't know was very uncomfortable. Especially in the quote unquote crazy house! I didn't want to go to sleep so I stood in the frame of the door, looking down the hall while listening to my roommate snore away. Out of nowhere a woman appeared in front of me. Almost like she just crept up on me like a ghost.

She was wearing a long white T-shirt that was see-through, and I could tell she wasn't wearing anything under it. In a very seductive and enticing voice, she asked me if it was my first night there. I swear it was the Devil! I told her, yeah, why. It was as though the Devil was still busy trying to entice me into some kind of trap, or there to continue to inject fear into my mind. With a devilish grin, she asked me how I was feeling so far. I gave her my famous line, I'm all right.

Then in a very demonic tone, she said, "Well, we will see how you doing by the end of the night." She then walked into her room right across the hall from mine leaving her door opened and laid across her bed, looking at me. It was some freaky shit going on! I mean it was like the exorcist!

There was no way I was going to sleep after that! What did she mean by "we'll see by the end of the night"? I stood watch, continuing to stand in the doorway. After a while a nurse came to me and said, "You must be David."

I told her yes, and she told me that I had to go to sleep. I said, "Naw, I'm cool."

She said OK and walked away after closing that ladies door while she was still laying in the bed eyeballing me until the door completely shut.

The nurse shortly returned with a glass of water and some pills for me to take. I assumed they were to make me go to sleep. Keep in mind I just took a whole bottle of sleeping pills only days ago, and a glass of water and more sleeping pills was the last thing I wanted to see. I didn't want to take them, but she made it very clear that I was going to. I took them, and she made me open my mouth to make sure that I swallowed them, and after that she left.

I continued to stand in the doorway and had convinced myself that I was going to be strong and that if I had to stand there all night, I would. I wasn't going to sleep at all. Well, let's just say that those must have been some powerful pills. I woke up the next morning in bed, tucked in nicely under the covers with no recollection on how I got there.

I got out of the bed and walked over to the doorway, trying to remember what happened and how I got from the doorway to the bed, but I couldn't remember. I looked down the long hallway toward the dreaded double doors that locked me in when I got there. To my surprise that same lady that was wearing the see-through T-shirt before I passed out was now fully dressed and looked back at me while walking right out of the unit. *How weird,* I thought. *This place is crazy.* And I never saw her again.

I then noticed that my roommate was waking up. He was an old, grumpy dude. He woke up, mumbling and fusing to himself and passing gas very loudly as he proceeded to the bathroom. All I could think was, *How did I get here?* You know what I'm saying? I mean I knew how I got there, but man, this whole experience was mind-blowing! Then I heard someone yell, "Breakfast!"

CHAPTER 8

# The Koo Koo's Nest

• • •

STILL DRESSED IN HOSPITAL ATTIRE, I began to walk down the hallway into the dining room. I noticed something different about my walk. Due to all of the trauma I had caused my body and to a reaction I was having to the medication they currently had me on, my muscles were very tense and stiff. Causing me to walk very slowly, hunched over, and my right arm would not relax. Every time I would force my right arm down to my side with my left hand, it would slowly rise back up again like into the shape of an *L*.

I was walking so slowly it seemed liked I would never get down that hallway to eat. The break room seemed so far away as I slowly crept down the hall, watching the other patients pass me by. Everything was moving in slow motion.

When I finally reached the break room, I noticed that all the patients were lined up in a single-file line. The first assignment of the day was to have your vitals taken and for you to have your medication. One patient after another. Hurry, hurry, step right up and get your fix for the day. Blood pressure checked, heart rate checked, and meds. I got in line and waited my turn. When the time came, they strapped my arm in the blood pressure cup, listened to my heart rate, gave me more pills, and sent me on my way. All I could think was, *Boy, you in the nuthouse now. They gonna stuff ya full of meds, and you'll be a zombie soon.*

After I was all checked out, I went to go sit down. The dining room consisted of about six to seven eight-foot tables with chairs around on both sides. I really didn't want to sit by anyone, so I went to an empty table and sat alone, waiting on my food. I began to look around the room at all of the different patients that were there. There were a wide range of ages and races. This was the first time that I got to see nearly all of the patients that were on the unit. I'd seen at least twenty to thirty all together. It was so weird and nerve-racking to be in there with them.

As I look back on it now, I remember my senses being very sensitive at this time. Certain sounds would absolutely drive me crazy. Like hearing the ice machine grind when someone was getting a cup of ice. Or the sound of chairs being scooted around on the floor, sounding like fingernails on a chalkboard. I was even tuned into the hands on the clock, tick and tock. I was going insane! I was feeling a pressure in my head that was totally new to me. It felt like I had to learn my senses all over again, like it was my first time hearing, tasting, touching, seeing, or smelling.

Soon one of the nurses rolled in a large metal cabinet that held all of the patients meals. The nurse began to call each patient's name so they could come and retrieve their tray. One by one they retrieved their breakfast. Due to medical reasons, everyone wasn't getting the same things to eat. Some had high blood pressure, others were diabetics, allergic to this, allergic to that. I was starting to realize that I was in the midst of some really sick people here. Not yet accepting that I was one of them.

My name was called, and I got up to go get my tray. On the way back to the table, I heard one of the patients repeat my name out loud. It was an older man, slim, bald, and very pale, and he had scabs and sores on him. I couldn't tell what was wrong with him, but he looked very sickly. "Dave," he repeated, giggling this time, reminding me of the Crypt Keeper. I gave no response as I took my seat. A few others tried to talk to me, but I kept my talk very minimal and short.

After I was done eating one of the nurses told me to check the chalkboard for the schedule for the day before I went back to my room. It was a list of all the times of different activities that would take place throughout the week. I took a look and walked to my room. While walking to my room, one of the nurses yelled out for smoke break. He began to hand each patient their packs of cigarettes. One by one they ran to get them as he called out the different brands. They were so excited.

GROUP SCHEDULE
3 NORTH

| | Monday | Tuesday | Wednesday | Thursday | Friday | Saturday | Sunday |
|---|---|---|---|---|---|---|---|
| 700 - 800 | ADL's Breakfast | ADL's Breakfast | ADL's Breakfast | ADL's Breakfast | ADL's Breakfast | ADL's Breakfast | ADL's Breakfast |
| 800 - 815 | Smoke Break | Smoke Break | Smoke Break | Smoke Break | Smoke Break | Smoke Break | Smoke Break |
| 830 - 900 | MHT/Goals Groups | MHT/Goals Groups | MHT/Goals Groups | MHT/Goals Groups | MHT/Goals Groups | MHT/Goals Groups | MHT/Goals Groups |
| 900 - 950 | Group Therapy | Group Therapy | Group Therapy | Group Therapy | Group Therapy | S / S Group | Exercise |
| 950 - 1000 | Snacks | Snacks | Snacks | Snacks | Snacks | Snacks | Snacks |
| 1000 - 1030 | Exercise | Exercise | Exercise | Exercise | Exercise | GroupTherapy 10:00 - 11:00 | GroupTherapy 10:00 - 11:00 |
| 1100 - 1115 | Smoke Break | Smoke Break | Smoke Break | Smoke Break | Smoke Break | Smoke Break | Smoke Break |
| 1115 - 1200 | Healthy Living Group | Spirituality Group | Games | Cooking Group | Healthy Living Group | Stress Management | Bingo |
| 1200 - 100 | Lunch Time | Lunch Time | Lunch Time | Lunch Time | Lunch Time | Lunch Time | Lunch Time |
| 100 - 115 | Smoke Break | Smoke Break | Smoke Break | Smoke Break | Smoke Break | Smoke Break | Smoke Break |
| 130 - 200 | Fitness Walk | Fitness Walk | Fitness Walk | Fitness Walk | Fitness Walk | Fitness Walk 130 - 200 | Fitness Walk 130 - 200 |
| | | | | | | Visitation 200 - 400 | Visitation 200 - 400 |
| 230 - 330 | Crafts | Crafts | Crafts | Crafts | Crafts | 200 - 400 | 200 - 400 |
| 345 - 400 | Smoke Break | Smoke Break | Smoke Break | Smoke Break | Smoke Break | Smoke Break | Smoke Break |
| 400 - 500 | MHT Group | MHT Group | MHT Group | MHT Group | MHT Group | MHT Group | MHT Group |
| 500 - 600 | Dinner | Dinner | Dinner | Dinner | Dinner | Dinner | Dinner |
| 600 - 615 | Smoke Break | Smoke Break | Smoke Break | Smoke Break | Smoke Break | Smoke Break | Smoke Break |
| 600 - 800 | Visitation | Visitation | Visitation | Visitation | Visitation | Visitation | Visitation |
| 815 - 900 | Smoke Break/ Snacks | Smoke Break/ Snacks | Smoke Break/ Snacks | Smoke Break/ Snacks | Smoke Break/ Snacks | Smoke Break/ Snacks | Smoke Break/ Snacks |
| 900 - 1030 | Games | Games | Games | Games | Games | Games | Games |
| 1030 | Socializing | Socializing | Socializing | Socializing | Socializing | Socializing | Socializing |
| 1130 | Bedtime | Bedtime | Bedtime | Bedtime | Bedtime | Bedtime | Bedtime |

Revised 7-12-03

My new schedule.

62

This brought to my attention the different things we do to harm our own selves. The addiction to cigarettes is no less than the addiction to drugs, sex, or alcohol. The nurse asked me if I wanted to go on the break, and I told him, no, I didn't smoke. He told me that I could use it as a chance to go outside and get some fresh air. I told him that I would pass. I wasn't really ready to go outside yet. All I could think was who would see me, or who would I see out there. I wasn't ready to face anyone.

I took this opportunity to use the phone and call home to my mother. Immediately I began to plead and beg for her to come and get me. She told me that it was out of her control and they couldn't come. A silence fell upon me. It was here that the Devil continued to mess with my mind. While my mom was talking to me, my mind drifted away, and I zoned off. I could still hear my mother, but that Spirit of Suicide began to speak again saying, "You're never going home! You're locked up. You're in the crazy house." I really began to believe that I wasn't ever going home again! With all my heart, I believed that this was where they put you for doing this kind of thing and I was never going to be allowed to go home.

When I came back to my senses, my mom encouraged me to hang in there and that she would come visit me during visiting hours. She asked me if there was anything that I wanted from my house. All I wanted was my Bible. Have you ever had a particular Bible that really meant a lot to you? You know that one special Bible that for some reason seemed to have more power than the others! That one that brought you and your family through all kinds of stuff growing up! The one with all the miles on it! It got all the highlights from sermons over the years! Get the point! My mom and I had a Bible that we used together while I was growing up. I can recall many nights as a child that I would go into my mother's room and she would be reading from it. I would crawl up into bed with her, and we would read from it together. Over the years this Bible for me proved to be that choice Bible for our family. As time passed it was left around and landed in my possession. I cherished it dearly and used it quite often.

I made sure that she would bring it to me, and she assured me that she would. We told each other we loved each other, and we got off the phone. I sat there for a minute, took a look at my new surroundings, took a deep breath, and accepted that I was never going home again. Then I got up walked down the hallway, up the driveway, across the sidewalk, on to the front porch of my room. My new home!

## THE COURTROOM OF THE MIND

After returning to my room, I noticed that my roommate was no longer there. He got discharged, and all of his things were gone. You would have thought that this would have given me a clue that one day I would get out also, but it didn't. I was just glad to have a room to myself. The Devil had me really fooled into thinking that I was never getting out.

I laid on the bed, staring at the ceiling and the four walls that continued to close in on me. As I sat there, I began to determine that all of my failures and mistakes qualified me to be in this situation. I fell deeper into my depression as I analyzed my life and all the wrongs I had done. Magnifying my mistakes over and over again. Rewinding and fast-forwarding episodes of my life in my mind, blaming and judging myself. Examining the evidence on why I was feeling that I deserved to be where I was, forever. This is when I entered into the courtroom of the mind!

The dictionary defines the plaintiff as a person who brings a case against another in a court of law. It defines the defendant as the accused in a court of law. It also defines the judge as one appointed to give a verdict in a court of law. The gavel sounds! All rise! You have just entered the courtroom of the mind. Insert *The People's Court* theme music here, and the drama begins!

In the courtroom of the mind, you play all three roles, the plaintiff, defendant, and the judge. You are the defendant that stands before yourself, the judge. While you the plaintiff begins with your opening arguments. "Your Honor, I will prove to you that the defendant has proven themselves to be the worst person in the history of mankind! The defendant is no longer worthy to walk the face of the earth! The defendant's poor choices and bad decisions in life have been unlike no other person in the world! I am asking you to lay down the law with vengeance and malice with the stiffest of all punishments, the death sentence!" The sound of a deep gasp of air from witnesses fills the courtroom with astonishment!

"Order in the court! Order in the court!" the judge says while the plaintiff takes his seat.

The courtroom is dead silent! You could hear a pin drop! After listening to the plaintiff, the defendant cannot believe what he was hearing. As his blood begin to boil, he had heard enough. He slams his handcuffed hands onto the table and rises up! He tries to wipe the sweat from his brow but can't because of the shackles connecting his feet to his handcuffs. He opens his mouth to speak and says...nothing, as the sweat and tears begin to pour down his face. The embarrassment and shame won't allow the defendant to even defend himself. His mind won't let him. In this state he can't see any of the positive things about himself. He can only magnify the negative ones.

"Do you have anything to say for yourself?" the judge asks.

"No, your Honor," the defendant says. Now silenced, the defendant becomes a mere spectator in the courtroom of the mind and sits back and listens to the trial.

"You may call your first witness," the judge tells the plaintiff.

"Thank you, your Honor, but I only have one witness to call I would like to call the defendant to the stand!"

The defendant takes the stand, is sworn in, and promises to tell the truth, the whole truth, and nothing but the truth!

In the courtroom of the mind, you can try, but you can't lie to yourself. This is where you begin to look at all of the negative things about you that you don't like. Those negative things that everyone knows about you, and also the ones that you think no one else knows about. The mind deceives you into believing that no one else has ever gone through some of the same things that you have, and that even if they have, your circumstance has to be the worst-case scenario.

The plaintiff approaches the stand to begin questioning from their long list of accusations. "This won't take long, your Honor. Trust me," the plaintiff brags. It's an open and closed book case, a no brainer! Shall we take a walk down memory lane?

We begin this story with a young man whose mother did the best she could do to raise him up properly in a broken home! At an early age, he showed great promise, blessed with many gifts and talents but without proper guidance knew not the right path to channel them in. Searching for acceptance and appreciation as most children growing up in a single-parent home often do, he found himself desiring to be in the "In Crowd," the who's who among his peers.

Blessed with the gift of being able to make one laugh and smile, he was able to woo his way into the hearts of the "Middle Crowd." The not all the way in but not all the way out crowd. Not knowing that this can also a be a very damaging place to be in as well. You see, when you're in and accepted, you're in! When you're out, you're out! At least you know where you stand. When you find yourself in the middle crowd, you become an entertainer, trying to get in the in and look like you're above the out. A wavering position to be in because although at times feeling the acceptance from the in crowd, quite often hurtfully you're reminded that you're not. Never realizing that everyone is trying to make it one step up in the social order of society, even the people that you feel are in the in. Those people can't fully accept you for the fear of losing their acceptance of the people that they feel are above you in the social order. Therefore you never know who your true friends are, failing to realize that all the time you were always in the "Out Crowd."

"This condition caused the defendant to become a people pleaser, your Honor. Worried more so with what others thought of him and his decisions rather than realizing who he was and accepting himself as an individual. Never learning how to love himself as the person God had created him to be spiraled himself into countless acts of recklessness and endangerment. Beginning with the rebellion of discipline, lack of self-discipline. Into lusting of the eyes by ways of pornography at a early age, continuing into fornication, leading to children out of wedlock. On to being a part of child abortion decisions. Dibble and dabbling with drugs and alcohol. Dishonoring his commitment of marriage to God, his wife, and family with the ultimate betrayal of adultery, and now suicide! Do we really need to go any further, your Honor?"

Upon hearing every accusation place upon him, the defendant realizes that death doesn't seem too much of a cruel punishment for a person with such credentials. "Do you have anything to say for yourself?" the plaintiff asks.

"No," the defendant shamefully responds.

"Then I rest my case, your Honor," says the plaintiff.

"You may be seated," the judge says to the defendant.

After the defendant takes his seat, the judge calls for him to call his first witness. The defendant remains silent, seated in a daze, thinking about his life up til now and all of the mistakes he's made that the plaintiff pointed out. All the hurt and damage he had caused to himself as well as others. The judge bangs the gavel down repeatedly! "Call your first witness, defendant!" the judge says forcefully.

The loud sounds from the gavel awaken the defendant out of his daze. He realizes he's definitely in a bind and surely will be condemned. He's not prepared for this case and has no witnesses to help with his defense. He rises from his seat and says, "Your Honor, the plaintiff is right on all charges brought before you. I'm guilty of all of them, and I'm sure plenty more! So go ahead. Throw the book at me. I deserve it!" He gives up on himself and says, "Your Honor, the defense res—"

But, before the defendant could finish his statement of resting his case, an unknown person burst into the courtroom, disrupting everything, and mayhem breaks loose. "Order in the court," the judge says as he bangs the gavel again. As the unknown guest approaches the front of the courtroom. The judge asks him to announce who he is.

"My name is Jesus. I'm here on behalf of the defendant. I am the court-appointed lawyer for him. Please excuse me for my tardiness. I just finished another case."

"Oh, so you're Jesus," the judge says. "I've heard of you. The lawyer that always shows up right on time! Your reputation proceeds yourself. Well, it looks like you've done it again, for I was just about to close the book on this one."

"May I have time to counsel with my client?" Jesus says.

"I object, your Honor," the plaintiff yells. "This is turning into a circus. This should be over!" the plaintiff yells once more.

"Quiet down, counsel, before I charge you with contempt of court," the Judge says to the plaintiff. "Granted," the judge says. "We will take a short recess for counsel to meet with the defendant and then pick up where we left off." The gavel sounds for recess as the plaintiff begins to sweat and tremble in fear while looking at Jesus.

The defendant turns to Jesus and asks, "What are you doing here again? Don't you think that you should just give up on me? Besides, I've tried you too many times, and here I sit again!"

Jesus smiles and says, "My child, haven't you figured it out yet? There's nothing that you can do that will allow me to turn my back on you! Now just relax and let me get you out of this mess once again."

As the court comes back into session, the judge tells Jesus to present his case. "Well, your Honor," Jesus says. Over two thousand years ago, I came to set the captive free. I gave my life so the defendant would not have to give his. I laid my life down to atone for all sin of mankind. So he who is without sin cast the first stone." The plantiff hangs his head. "I was crucified, and I died for the defendant that he may have life and live. He will not die. I rose again and have returned with the keys of life and death, and with those keys, I'm here to unlock the chains that are around my client. No more judging, no more condemning."

And just like that, I was free, and so are you. Case dismissed. Forgive yourself and walk out of that courtroom in your mind a new person with a new lease on life. Who the son sets free is free indeed!

## CHAPTER 9

# Looney Tunes... What's Up, Don?

• • •

Now back in my room from breakfast, I looked at myself in the plastic mirror in my room. Yeah, plastic so you couldn't break it and cut yourself with it. I was looking bad, I tell ya. I had not shaved, my hair wasn't combed, I was musty, and still dressed in hospital clothes.

Nevertheless, I was grateful! Although the Devil had me convinced that I was never getting out, I began to just thank God for sparing my life. If this was where I had to be, then so be it. I knew that it could be a lot worse than this. I found comfort in being away from the outside world. I looked at it as though the outside world was the real crazy house, and I was glad to be away from it all. So I accepted my new home and began to decide how I could make it more comfortable for me. I thought if I was going to be there, I might as well make it as comfortable as possible for me.

I started looking at my patient wristbands. You know the plastic ones with your name, the doctor's name, and other info on it. Well, for some reason, it began to symbolize some kind of bondage for me, like handcuffs. I felt like I was someone else's property or something. Like I wasn't my own and I belonged to the state. I guess I did, though. Immediately I wanted them taken off. I began pulling and pulling but couldn't get them off. I went to the nurses station and asked if she could cut them off, and she told me no. I couldn't get them off until the doctor okayed it. The little strength that I was gaining from the thought of being able to break out these handcuffs would have to wait.

It was time for my first group session. They called all the patients in to the dining room. There was a lady sitting in the front of the room. She introduced herself to all of the new patients. I can't really recall what she talked about, so I don't want to make up anything. But I do remember just looking around at all of the patients and seeing why some of them were there. I saw bandages wrapped around some of their wrists. I saw what looked like hard-core drug addicts, so at least I thought. Others were completely basket cases, mumbling, slobbering, and talking to themselves in their own little world.

I do remember the instructor talking about depression, and it being a illness. I never looked at it like that. I had no clue how severe depression was for some people. It's actually a real sickness. Major depression is very hard to deal with. As a people we all go through many different things and challenges, but for some it's hard to process disappointments and know how to deal with them and get past them. It's real easy to just say you'll get over it to someone, especially if you're a very strong person. For others it's not quite that simple.

I remember one young lady talking about how she was abused and made fun of all her life. She walked with a limp because she had polio in one of her legs. She raised up her pants leg and showed it to us. I'd heard of polio before but never knew what it was or the effects of it. Let's just say it looked like someone had taken an ice cream scoop and had scooped out little scoops of her leg all over it. She was very short and was on the heavy side, I'll say, but had the brightest smile and long, beautiful black hair down her back. She was so sweet. I remember her also raising up her sleeve, showing her whole arm where she had taken a shotgun and shot herself in the shoulder at some point of her life. It looked like one huge burn of melted flesh twisting and meshing its self together as it healed. It seemed horrible.

I found out I was diagnosed with major depression, signs of being bipolar, and mild schizophrenic tendencies. I didnt know what any of that meant, but I refused to accept it from day one. True, I had tried to commit suicide. True, I was depressed. Maybe I may had talked to myself in my head a bit. Who hasn't talked to them selves and heard their conscious talk back to them in some way? I refused to accept the fact that I was sick. In my mind I had had a little breakdown. I made it through it, it's over, and I'm not suppose to be here with these people! That was my story, and I was sticking to it!

After group it was time for snacks, and then on to exercise. A new instructor gathered us in the den area, forming a circle of chairs. Now keep in mind this was a group of a lot of different ages, and I was one of the younger ones. We all sat down, and they began a warm-up. I thought to myself, *So we warming up sitting down in chairs, OK!* Then she started playing some music. Music from the '60s and '70s like "Twist and Shout," then "You Sexy Thing" by Hot Chocolate. "I believe in miracles, you sexy thing," is how the song went!

Then something weird started happening to me. I'm not sure if I can really explain it, though. The instructor went into her routine. I mean she was really into it, too. Imagine it, we were sitting, down raising our arms up and down, marching in place, bending from side to side. One and two and one and two! *Am I in a nursing home or something?* I thought. *LOL!* That pressure was building in my head again. I began to get achy, and my vision was getting blurry! It felt like I was going to faint. I was holding my head with both hands! Then she played "Play That Funky Music, White Boy"! I was about to lose my mind! LOL! *Not again,* I thought! The other patients were fine! They were bouncing around in their chairs, moving left to right just laughing away, having fun! I couldn't handle the site of it any longer! *Am I on* Punk'd! I thought it was a joke that they was playing on me, and it wasn't funny at all. I got up, still holding my head, and walked to a corner of the room! It was too much! The instructor came over and asked me what was wrong. I really didn't know!

She excused me to my room, so that's where I went. The other patients went off on their ways to the infamous smoke break. While in my room, I tried to figure out what was going on with me. It was a feeling that I wasn't use to at all, but it was somewhat familiar to me. It was some of the same feelings that I had when this crazy week first started. The feeling of fear, being boxed in, nervous, embarrassed, and unsure. I was having what I know now to be a panic attack of some sort. I'd never experienced anything like it before in my life up until then. *Maybe I am sick,* I began thinking.

After I laid down for a while, it was time for lunch. I was still in an anxious state of mind and really didn't want to be bothered. It was the same routine, wait for your name to be called and get your tray. My named was called, and for some reason the old man from breakfast started saying my name again! "Dave, Dave, Dave!" I'd had enough. Up until then I'd hadn't talked much to any of the patients, but I knew his name.

I turned to him and said, "It's David, Don!" The room got real quiet! I guess they were in shock that I spoke to somebody. I remember Don had on a blue T-shirt that had Bugs Bunny on it. It was a Looney Toon shirt. LOL. How fitting right! It showed Bugs Bunny on it lifting weights, and it said something like, "You can do it." Message!

The brain is funny, I tell you. My senses were still acting funny, I guess, because whenever I said the name Don, my mind went to my high school baseball coach. His name was Don, so I guess hearing a familiar name triggered a memory. I remembered the day I went out for baseball. It was one day after school. I was waiting for my ride to pick me up. A friend of mine told me I should come out to baseball tryouts, since I was just sitting around waiting. So off I went to the baseball field. Everyone was taking a turn at bat while also playing in the field when it wasn't his turn to hit. Coach was on the mound. Soon as I walked up, some one was off to take his turn in the field, and everyone was like, "Get up there, David!" So I walked on up and gave it a shot! I grabbed a bat with all the confidence in the world, and *boom*. Strike one! Pow, strike two!

Coach said, "Son, I don't think baseball's your sport!" With that came a curveball that I thought was going to hit my head, I ducked and strike three!

By that time I knew my ride was in the front of the school, waiting on me, and I probably was in trouble for having them waiting so I took off. All the way home, all I could think about was, "Son, I don't think baseball's your sport." It would not leave my head. Although a little hurtful to the ego, it was encouraging. So by the end of the evening, I told my mom that I would be coming home late, and I was going to baseball practice again! I had something to prove! He didn't know who he was talking too! LOL.

Over the course of a few practices, I was on the team! Not too great, but coach seen my determination and thought I had potential. It felt great to get that uniform and be a part of something. I thought my baseball hat was the best thing going, I tell ya! I turned out to be a pretty decent outfielder. Needless to say by midseason I was starting a lot of games and was a pretty good pinch hitter when the team was in a slump and needed a rally!

*Son, I don't think baseball's your sport.* Now I could have took that statement and tucked my tail and never came back out for practice. Thinking about all of this, I realized something. That was what I had done when I tried to commit suicide. The Spirit of Suicide said, "Son, I don't think life is your sport." I tucked my tail and decided not to return to practice, to life. I saw the curveball coming straight for my head and gave myself strike three! Death, you're out!

After that I began to get even stronger. I still had something to prove, but not to coach but to myself. Just like I made the team, I could make the team of life as well. Every time I would see Don, he would have on that Looney Toon shirt. I would see Bugs Bunny lifting weights saying, "You can do it." Giving me the same encouragement that my coach gave me. Passing Don daily in the halls with that shirt on became funny and encouraging to me. It's funny how lessons are set up for us to learn long before we get the point. Never give up on yourself! You can do it! Sure, life throws us all some curveballs. You may even go down swinging, but if you don't give up, you'll have another opportunity to step back up to the plate! Another chance at bat! Thanks, Coach Don! Both of you.

Once lunch was over again, it was time for the infamous smoke break! Boy, they went crazy for them smoke breaks! Although a bit stronger, I still wasn't ready to go outside yet, so I just sat around in the den. One of the patients started talking to the nurse at the front desk and telling her how pretty a vase of flowers were on the counter. I heard her say that they were from my mom. My mom had given it to the nurses for taking good care of me. My mom was a nurse as well and had taken good care of so many people, and she was appreciative of getting the same good care and treatment in her time of need. The flowers made me feel like she was there with me every time I saw them while passing the nursing station. That also made me stronger. I began to open up and talk to a couple of the patients, and made a few friends.

It was now time for a fitness walk. I thought it was outside, so at first I didn't want to go. Then I was told that it was inside the hospital in an exercise room. I was a little nervous about going, but I went anyway. This was actually my first time off the floor. The dreaded double doors opened, and I was on my way. My body was still sore and stiff, and I was still walking very slowly.

After making our way down the elevator, we were escorted by nurses down a hallway into a room. It was like a small gym. A rehab room, I would say. There were exercise bikes, exercise games to play like ring tossing. People were also playing ping-pong and catch. It was a safe room. All the equipment, walls, and toys were like nerf foam so you couldn't hurt yourself. The room had padded walls and carpet with track lanes imprinted along the outer portion. There were patients from other floors there as well. I walked around the track slow as a turtle. I didn't talk to anyone. I just did a few laps. I remember seeing a guy with a brace on his head walking the track. It looked like he had broken his neck or something. It appeared very painful. You could see screws going into his skull. I wanted to ask him what happened to him, but I didn't. Although in the days that followed, I found out that he had shot himself in the head. I was really being exposed to some hurting people.

It was good to get off the unit for a while. Upon returning it was time for arts and crafts. I had taken pride in knowing I was a good artist, at least at one point of my life. I had put the pencil and pad down for quite some time now. I thought I might get a chance to catch up on my skills, until we were given a coloring book and crayons! LOL! What the! Are they serious? I mean they were for-real colorings books, too! Like for three year olds! Connect the numbers to make a picture and then color it in type stuff! LOL! It made me smile, and I think I had my first laugh! So what did I do? I colored! Believe it or not, it was very relaxing, and the room was quite for the first time, just like intense little kids in coloring class! Except we were all grown. LOL! It really is funny as I type this, thinking back on it.

It was almost time for my first visiting hour. I was looking forward to seeing my family. What was that going to be like? After another infamous smoke break, group session, and dinner, it was time.

I was sitting in my room, and I remember someone coming in and telling me that my family was here. I began to make my way down the hallway to the dining hall. I was still walking very slow, and my arm still would not go down. They were so happy to see me, and as well I was happy to see them. They joked with me about how slow I was walking and my arm, and it was good to laugh, so I didn't mind.

One thing that I noticed was that my family was one of the only families that was there for visiting hours. All these people and no one was there to see them. It was kinda sad. Another sign for me to be grateful. I couldn't have imagined going through something like this all alone. We all sat around the table and took turns reading scriptures and praying. I wasn't allowed to see my kids because kids were not allowed on the unit. Which was fine because even I thought I was I wasn't mentally ready to see them yet. They would only allow me two visitors at a time at first, so my family had to rotate in and out.

I remember while my sister was in with me, one of the patients came in and started moving the chairs around. There was nobody in there but us. It was that lady from the first night that was running around saying, "I'm a write my daddy a letter." Her name was Sarah. She was playing musical chairs all by herself, scooting the chairs around on the floor, making a lot of noise. My sister and I just looked at her rearrange the whole room while talking to herself in amazement.

I turned to my sister with a face of disbelief and disgust and said, "And so I'm supposed to be in here, right? This is where y'all got me."

She didn't know what to say. The noise of those chairs scooting around on the floor was driving me crazy, so I yelled, "Sarah, get out of here!" And she stopped and left.

My family had brought me my Bible, sanitary supplies, some get well soon cards from friends and family, and a few new outfits from a friend of mine's clothing store. East Coast Wear, a urban clothing store that carried all the latest in urban hip-hop fashion. Phat Farm, Sean John, Timberlands, Clark's, Akedemics, Roca Wear, Mecca, and plenty more. It was owned by a Jamaican cat, who was truly a good friend to everybody in the community. Believe it or not, Oklahoma is one big melting pot. You might be surprised to know that there are quite a number of Jamaicans, Africans, as well as other ethnic groups in Oklahoma. (Shout out to the Queen of Sheba Restaurant and Reggae Night.)

Sosa always had good wisdom and good advice for me if I had a issue that I wanted to talk about. He always encouraged me to keep doing my thing, stay positive, and one day I would get the results I wanted in my business. See he was a young entrepreneur as well, who understood the struggles of running a small business in a small market like Oklahoma.

Getting those clothes helped me a lot. It let me escape my locked-up situation and led me straight to the Jamaican and Bob Marley vibes of East Coast Wear. I could see Sosa saying, "Man, hang in there. Wat cha you doing, D—with that Jamaican accent and tree root in his mouth, LOL!—"I told you God got a plan for you and what's yours will be yours." It made me realize that I had people in my corner despite the naysayers and the haters out there. I just needed to figure out who was who because I really didn't know anymore.

My family and I said our good-byes as I escorted them to the dreaded double doors. With fresh new gear Sosa sent me and Bible in hand. Again I watched through the windows of the locked doors as they entered the elevator. While I made my way back home down the hallway.

# CHAPTER 10

# Hide-and-Seek

• • •

BY NOW I WAS READY to take a shower and get out of those hospital clothes. The shower and the laundry room were right next to my room. So I gathered my fresh new gear along with my fresh new kicks that my family brought to me as well. A fresh new pair of tennis shoes could always brighten my day, even if they were from Walmart and fully equipped with Velcro to fasten them up. You weren't allowed to have shoestrings, for safety reasons. Boy, they thought of everything, I tell ya. Everything right down to your shoestrings. LOL!

It was my first shower! I'm here to tell ya that was the best shower I'd ever had! At first it was a little uncomfortable because I was thinking that there was a hidden camera in there so they could monitor you, even in the shower. Hey, why not? Security was tight on every other level. I bet it was in there, too!

Eventually I relaxed and enjoyed my shower. I had already woken up to a cathather in me a couple of days ago, so what else was there for anybody to see! If there were a camera in there, then so be it. I sat down in the handicap chair and let the water just run all over me! Ahhhhhhhhh! A nice, warm shower! I didnt want to leave.

After my skin began to wrinkle like I had been swimming all day, I dried off. I put on my fresh new drawers, undershirt, new outfit, and returned to my room. I got to brush my teeth and comb my hair as well. I was told that I could have someone give me a shave if I wanted, but I passed on that. Guess I didn't trust no one in there with a razor to my face, not even the staff.

I began to think, look at all the little things we take for granted every day. Warm water to take a shower with. A roof over your head to brush your teeth in. There are so many people out there whose situations are worse off than yours. Homeless, nowhere to go! No family to bring them fresh new gear! I started feeling like a spoiled, unappreciative kid. As I stared at myself in the mirror, I realized that there was someone out there who would change lives with me in a heartbeat, even though I was in a psychiatric ward.

Over the next few days, I spent a lot of time looking out of the windows, trying to figure out where I was in the city—which I never did figure out until I got out—and doing a lot of reflecting. It was weird looking from the inside out. I hadn't been outside in about a week. The airplanes flying in the sky teased me into wanting to escape with them. While looking out of the windows, looking at all of the different cars go by, I thought of different people that matched the car I saw. One in particular I saw quite a bit and kept me encouraged. A delivery truck from a local linen company called Commercial Linen. I had a delivery guy named Ray that worked for this company that delivered towels to my shop. He was a very positive and encouraging dude. We often shared stories of our past and how God saw us through a lot of situations in our lives. Seeing that truck move around outside every day gave me hope and reminded me of all the good, positive conversations we had shared. God was using people to encourage me, and they had no idea. You never know how your life can be used as a reflection of God's light to encourage someone. Always remember that.

I stayed in prayer and read my word daily, growing stronger and stronger by the days. Eventually after a group session with my doctor, I was cleared to take off my handcuffs (the name tag wristbands).

While on the unit, I always carried my Bible. One day a nurse stopped me in the hallway and told me she had a scripture for me. It was **Jeremiah 29:11. It reads, "'For I know the plans I have for you,' declares the Lord, 'plans to prosper you and not harm you, plans to give you hope and a future.'"** She encouraged me to hang in there and that God had a plan for all of this.

I held on to that thought and really drew nearer to God. I began to believe that God simply wanted to sit me down and get me to himself. Away from the disappointments, stresses, and bills. A place where all I could do was focus on him. There's a **Psalms 27:5 that says, "For in the time of trouble, he shall hide me."** In the mist of all the confusion that was going on in my life, God just simply wanted to play hide-and-seek! LOL!

Now we all know how the game is played. You count to one hundred while a friend goes and hides. After you are done counting, you set off to go find your friend. If you are successful in finding your friend, they become It and it's their turn to come and find you. If you aren't successful in finding your friend, and they get back to base safely, then they're safe and you are It again.

OK, bear with me on this one. I feel like I'm going somewhere with this. Let's break this down on a spiritual level. For in the time of trouble, he shall hide me. In the natural game of hide-and-seek you must hide yourself. Wouldn't it be great to have God hide you! I mean think about it, if you really needed a hiding place. A place away from trouble and danger, a place away from all of the stresses that we all deal with on a daily basis.

Who else would you want to hide you but God? Yourself? I don't think so. That's how most of us get into the trouble we get into anyhow, by trying to do things our own way. Sometimes we need God to even hide us from ourselves. There's a song by Pastor Bruce Parham called "Hide Me." It says,

> *"Lord, hide me in thy glory, in the secret place of your holiness and grace. That's where I worship in thy presence, bless your name, and give you reverence.*
>
> *Hide me where the hands of mercy covers me from the enemy. O' hide me from circumstance. Hide me when I want to take one more chance. I need you to hide me. When my strength is weak. Hide me when my eyes want to take one more glance.*
>
> *O' hide me. Lord, I need you to hide me. O' hide me. Hide me from the enemy. O' hide me. I need you to hide me. Lord, I'm asking you to hide me. O' hide me. Even if the enemy you hide is me."*

Sounds like a Song of David, go figure. That's a wonderful song, and I suggest it to everyone to listen to. It's so true that quit often that the "enemy" is the "inner me." Another way to look at this game of hide-and-seek that was brought to my attention, is that when you are in the world doing everything that you want to do, good or bad, God is presented to you and is very visual to you. God doesn't hide himself because he wants you to come to him and draw you closer. As children most of us grew up in church and pretty much have been introduced to God in some form or way. But something about this hide-and-seek thing is interesting to me. When the game begins, you choose a base, a safe place. Just the same as when you choose to begin your walk with God. Choosing to live a saved life is your base, your safe place to which you can always come back to for security.

The funny thing about this game of "Spiritual Hide-and-Seek" is that once you've made that decision to live a saved life, the real challenge comes into play. Now God seems to hide himself from you. Your journey begins, and it's time for you to seek him. Seek and you shall find! The thing is, God is still there all along. Through all the ups and downs. Through all the test and trials, God is right there. Sometimes it just doesn't feel like it. And just like in the natural game of hide-and-seek, if you don't find him the first time, you have another chance to find him again. The game is never over. Seek him daily!

As the days passed, I continued to walk closer and closer with the Lord. I stayed in my Bible constantly. I was gaining strength in the Lord quickly. One morning as I made my way down the hallway for breakfast, I stopped in the den area and the TV was on the news. It was a news report that the United States had just found and killed the sons of Sadam Houssain. They went on to show their faces all black and burned and pink with their skin peeling off. Immediately I thought, *Are we supposed to be happy about this? Are we supposed to be celebrating or something? This was someone's family, too, despite our objectives as a country!* My heart just began to hurt. I couldn't believe my eyes. Then the news went on to talk about a star college basketball player, Patrick Dennehy who'd been reported missing for about a month now. His body had been found. All the pain that was on the news was really affecting me, and I didn't want to believe any of it was true. I called home to see if they had seen the same reports, and they confirmed that indeed they were true. I was devastated! All the anxiety and pressure came rushing back! My body got stiff again! I started walking slow again, hunched over, back to my room, skipping breakfast. From that point on, my family asked me not to watch the news for a while.

Later on that evening, after visiting hours, I was sitting in the TV area, reading my Bible, and one of the patients said to me, "You know you can find all that 9/11 stuff in there?"

I asked her where, and she gave me a scripture. I can't recall what the scripture was, but it had nothing to do with 9/11 when I found it. I just laughed, but the thought of it being in the Bible was very interesting to me. So it sent me on a quest. I didn't know where to begin looking. So with me being in the mind-set that I was never getting out and had nothing but time on my hands to find it, I decided to just begin reading in the beginning, Genesis.

As I read through creation, the fall of man, and Noah and the flood, things became a little interesting to me. It began to speak about man building a tower to the heavens. The tallest tower they could build. And God coming down to see the tower, and from there God scattering them across the earth. Now of course it wasn't quite like 9/11, but the whole tall tower thing was interesting to me. I read through the night until I feel asleep.

Morning came, and while I sat on the edge of the bed, someone yelled for breakfast. By this time I had another roommate. He was still sleep, so I told him to get up for breakfast.

With a groggy voice, he said, "What time is it?"

He had a watch on his nightstand, so I looked at it, and my reply was, "It's 7:11. Time to wake up." Immediately, that phrase stuck in my head. "It's 7:11. Time to wake up." So I went over to my pen and pad and wrote it down, and then went on to breakfast. The whole time I was eating, that phrase kept playing itself over and over in my head. After breakfast I went back to my room, and this was the first poem (if you wanna call it that) I wrote after my suicide attempt.

# IT'S 7:11: TIME TO WAKE UP

*Time to wake up, world, America! For we are not living in the end times or the last days, but only the beginning. Genesis! If you look in Genesis, the scriptures have come to past. 9/11 can be found in Genesis chapter 11. Man had built the tallest towers they could build, and the Lord came down to see the tower and the city.*

*In **Genesis Chapter 13, it reads, Is not the whole land before you, separate? If you take the left hand, then I will take the right. If you take the right hand, then I will take the left.***

*Is the world not big enough for us all? We are in a war, fighting over land that is the Lord's anyway. God is calling for us all to turn from wickedness and evil doings and seek his face. We are in a battle that the outcome is already written.*

*We are all descendants of Noah and Abraham. In Genesis God scattered us all among the earth and confused our languages. God found favor in Noah and ordered him to take every clean animal and bird into the ark. The Lord is your ark.*

*We must turn to the Lord in these terrible times and become pure to establish God's clean church. See, most people would say that we are living in the last days. In T. D. Jakes's book,* Loose that Man and Let Him Go, *he states, "There is nothing like pain to bring forth a revelation."*

*As a country that is exactly what we are seeing, pain but we are living in the beginning. Are we not living in the days of Sodom and Gomorah, where the flesh of man was so strong. God said to Noah, "I have determined to make an end of all flesh, for the earth is filled with violence through them. I will destroy them with the earth."*

*God wants us to reestablish our covenant with him. We need world peace right now! In Genesis chapter 19 it talks about the warning to Sodom. Did America not warn Iraq before battle? America hit Iraq with everything it had, and is overthrowing the cites just as the scriptures read.*

*It is time for us all to put down the weapons and pray! Chapter 15 says as the sun was going down, a deep sleep feel on Abram. The sun is going down on America, and we don't even realize it. It also says that know of a surety that your descendant will be sojourners in a land that is not theirs and will be slaves there. We have Americans that are lost in a land they do not know, and in some cases have been taken prisoners.*

*We must put down the weapons and return to God's covenant.*

*Don't wait till it's too late.*

*Repent and turn from evil doing!*
*This is only the beginning, Not The End!*
*It's 7:11: Time to Wake Up!*

Now trust me as I look at it now I wouldn't say that I hit the nail on the head. I know I may have taken some scriptures the wrong way as well. Heck, I don't know! Some of you might be reading this and saying, "Yeah, you need to be in the crazy house." It was just crazy to me that there I was in the psychiatric ward, fresh off a suicide attempt, writing something like this. Although at the time, it did give me a new sense of worth. I felt like I had found a secret or a new revelation of some sort. All of the sudden, I had something to tell the world! It was my poem that would bring peace to the world, so I thought. I felt like if I were to send it to President Bush, I would get the Nobel Peace Prize or something! LOL! Needless to say I never sent it. I mean who was I at that point but a crazy man in the nuthouse, right?

Over the next few days, I began to share my newfound revelation with my family when they came to visit. I'm not sure if they thought I was crazy or what, LOL! They were just like, "Yeah, OK, that's interesting. LOL." They just continued to be in prayer for me, and we stayed in the word together.

I was a man on a mission from God now. I didn't know what the mission was, but I knew he had a plan for me, and that's all I needed! I had found a purpose that brought me encouragement, and sometimes that's all you need to press forward. I got to the point where when people would visit me, I would tell them simply, "Hey, I'm fine. This is all in God's plan for me. I'm supposed to be here!"

They would look at me kinda strange, like, "Yeah, right, look around you. You're not supposed to be here."

I knew I looked even crazier saying that, but I just knew that God would work this out for his good! I didn't know how, but I knew this would work out for my good! **Romans 8:28 says, "All things work together for good to them that love God, to them that are the called according to his purpose."** God had a purpose and plan for me.

I began waking up early every morning at six thirty to watch *The Potter's Touch*, with T. D. Jakes. I had the whole den to myself to worship because every one else was asleep. It became my daily routine. Jesus, Jakes, and coffee.

Soon all the patients on the floor began to see a change in me. Something was different to them about me! I was confident. I wasn't hunched over anymore! I began to laugh and smile again! I had gotten my joy back! Patients began to flock to me, even some of the nursing staff as well. They began to ask me to pray for them, and I would. They wanted to have Bible study with me, so I started asking my family to bring extra Bibles for the patients. I began praying and laying hands on patients and family right there on the unit! I was like I was having church in there.

We were seeing the whole unit change! Other patients began to be more confident and began to smile and laugh again! They loved to see my family come to visit. They didn't just come visit me. They spent time with everyone. It got to the point where one day this patient loved the dress my mother had and asked her for it. The next day my mom had it cleaned and gave it to her. Now I'm on the physc ward, watching a patient having fun, dancing, and spinning around in a dress that belonged to my mother! It was great. We brought life to the floor!

But wouldn't you know it, all of the sudden the powers that be put a stop to that. I was told that I was a patient and could no longer pray for other patients. Patients would have to check out Bibles from the patient library if they wanted a Bible. I was told that I couldn't influence anyone's spiritual beliefs in there. I didn't understand at first, but I followed the rules anyhow. I do get it now, though, although patients did make their way to my room for good night prayer sessions a couple times.

# CHAPTER 11

# Spirit Break

• • •

THE OTHER PATIENTS HAD THEIR smoke breaks, but I had what I called my spirit breaks. It was 6:30 a.m. Time to watch Jakes! While all the other patients were asleep, I was the only one up, watching *The Potter's Touch*, with Bishop T. D. Jakes. *The Potter's Touch* was definitely one of my saving graces while on the unit. It helped to give me the strength to face another day. One day while I watched, there was a commercial for a cruise coming up with T. D. Jakes. I just closed my eyes and thought of how wonderful that would be, to go on a cruise with Jakes and the Potter's House! I'd never been on a cruise before, and that sounded like the life for me! I wasn't even sure yet if I was ever getting out of the physc unit, but the thought of going was wonderful. I would see that commercial every day and wish that I could go.

I had not seen my kids up to this point yet, but it was around this time that I got clearance for them to visit. I had been begging to see them, and I was very excited! Kids were not allowed on the floor. So they allowed me to leave those dreaded double doors to sit in the lobby and visit them.

*Buzzzzzzz!* The doors opened, and there they were! My beautiful, wonderful children! Cameron, Isaiah, and Genesis, minus Mackenzie (Kenzie) because she lived out of the state. My beautiful, wonderful children! My beautiful, wonderful children!

Cam

Kenzie

Zay

Gen

What in the world was I thinking? How could I have left them to deal with that? They really didn't know what was going on. They just thought Daddy was sick. I could see the fear over both of my boys' faces. Their eyes were red from holding back the tears. They stood there both with a gift for me in their hands. Cam brought me a nice card that he drew himself! Zay brought me a little refrigerator magnet of the Incredible Hulk! Im sure that was his way of telling me to be strong. And my baby Gen! Lil Red! What can I say? That's just my baby girl! Cute as a button!

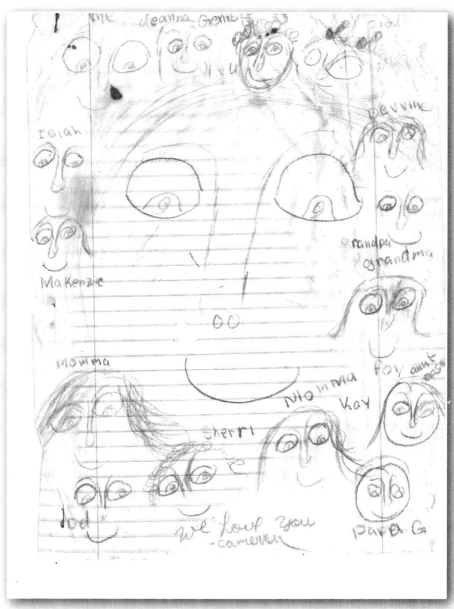

The hand-drawn card given to me by my son Cameron

All of the sudden, all the anxiety came rushing back again! The pressure built back up! I couldn't take it anymore! I think this is when reality really set in for me! *You actually just tried to kill yourself, man! How could you do that to your family and children?* I was so disappointed in myself, and the feeling was unbearable. I had to go back and lay down! I wasn't as ready to see them as I thought I was. It was just to much for me to handle. I was too ashamed of myself, so I buzzed the doors to let me back in after only about a five minutes into the visit at the most. It was too much.

I got back to my room and sat and thought about all of them and the responsibility I was leaving to their mothers, and I was ashamed of myself. I couldn't believe I did this to myself. I began to beat myself up all over again, until a nurse came to my room and told me it was time for smoke break. The infamous smoke break that everyone always rushed the halls to go to. She said she knew I didn't smoke, but it would be good for me to just go outside and get some air, so this time I did.

When we got down the elevators, we had to go through another unit's kitchen area to get outside. It seemed like an elderly unit. Nothing but older folks in wheelchairs. I remember there was this big black man in a wheelchair, and when he saw me, he yelled, "Big Isaiah!"

It made me think of my son. It encouraged me to get it together, stop beating myself up. I had to be strong and confident for both of my boys. I was like, "Yeah, I'm Big Isaiah," and I shook his hand.

When we got through the kitchen, there was a very big open courtyard for us to go outside and walk. I finally got to see the infamous smoke break area! It was outside, but it had a stockade fence around it so no one could see in and you couldn't see out. All this time I had been cooped up inside, worrying about who would see me, and there was a tall stockade fence. Go figure!

It was a nice courtyard to relax in. Lots of trees and flowers to look at. Park benches to sit down and enjoy the fresh air. I just walked all around and soaked it all in, and it did me some good to get outside and smell life again, besides the cigarette smoke. LOL.

In the days that followed, the infamous smoke break became one of my favorite times of the day as well! Instead of a smoke break, it was my spirit break! Just to go outside and feel the breeze and sun shining on my face made me appreciate still being alive. I just walked around and prayed and talked to God and thanked him for sparing my life. Funny how the one thing I didn't want to do turned out to be one of the best things for me. Life is kinda like that sometimes, right?

In the days to come, through my medication, my group sessions, exercise, prayer, and wonderful family and friend support, I was back on track. Growing stronger and stronger by the days. I was doing arts and crafts, making coffee, cleaning the break room, washing clothes, playing ping-pong, and eating three meals a day! Plus snacks! Hey, life ain't so bad! I could get use to this! Then wouldn't you know it? I got word that I was checking out!

# CHAPTER 12

# Time to Face the World

• • •

WELL, IT WAS TIME TO go! I never knew I was getting out! I knew some people were missing at times, but I just thought they were out for treatments or something. I think I was getting a little comfortable in there! LOL! Three meals a day when you've been struggling financially will do that to you!

It's crazy, but I got to meet some interesting people in there. You had your drunks, your drug addicts, abused, battered. People that had shot themselves, cut themselves, drug overdosed. People getting shock therapy. You name it, it was all there. Young, old, all races, and different economic backgrounds. Nobody was exempt. We were all the same, one big, happy family battling with a depression or mental illness of some kind.

They were all sad to see me go, and in some ways I was sad to leave them there. Not knowing what their futures would hold for them. The lady that was battling with extreme schizophrenia, Sarah, came over to me, gave me a hug, and mumbled in my ear, "My teacher," and gave me a picture she did in art class. I was really moved by that, and I'll never forget any of them. I thank God for them all and the staff there at St. Michael's Hospital.

Two weeks had past since my arrival into the unit. It was the longest two weeks of my life! It seemed like I had been in there forever. I gathered my things, took one last look at my room, and headed down the long hallway to those dreaded double doors! On my way to the doors, a nurse stopped me and said to me, "Don't ever let me see you in here again!"

I told her, "You won't." She buzzed the doors, and I was out. Free!

Actual picture given to me by Sarah

Down the elevator, I couldn't believe I was out. I was still walking a little stiff because of the medication, but I didn't care anymore who saw me! It was already all over the city what I had done anyway. Bad news always travels fast, right? So instead of thinking that I could hide it and keep my suicide a secret like most people do, I had no choice but to face the world head-on with it!

Driving home was weird because within those two weeks of looking out of windows, I never knew where I was or what side of town I was on. It took me a while to get my bearings. Ironically I was taken over to my mother's house, the exact same place where my journey started. She wanted me to stay with her so she could keep a close eye on me.

It was very weird to enter her home. It was like I was in a dream. Everything had happened right here. As I looked down the hallway, I could envision myself pacing back and forth. My first stop was right back into my grandmother's room where I took the bottle of pills. I stood in the doorway, looking at the bed and the nightstand.

I could see it all like it was happening all over again. My mom then went on to point out that the second bottle of pills that I took, that I had gotten from the kitchen cabinet was her prescription for asthma. The miracle in that was while the Tylenol PM was slowing my heart down her asthma medicine was speeding my heart up. Out of all the pills that were in the cabinet that I could have taken God orchestrated me to take an antidote. That was amazing to me, God was in control all along.

Then there I was, walking into my mom's office room where I had hid the second bottle of pills when I heard my uncle call my name. Then I walked into the back of the house where I passed out into the coma, my last recollection. I stood there and imagined how I must have looked, passed out on that couch. I couldn't imagine, though, how my mom must have felt seeing me there.

I hadn't shaved in weeks now, so you can imagine how rough the face was looking! LOL! I walked in the bathroom and just stared at myself in the mirror for a while. All kinds of thoughts were going through my head. I was so happy to still be alive. I took a shower, and I got the clippers out and gave myself a fresh cut and shave.

I continued to stay focused in my word and grew deeper in my prayer life. That allowed me to continue writing as well. Every other minute I was coming up with a new poem. I just couldn't stop writing! A buddy of mine use to tell me that his mother would always tell him, "Baby, don't get too far from the shore."

## DON'T GET TOO FAR FROM THE SHORE
### (DEDICATED TO WILLY B AND MOMMA SIMMS)

*When at the beach one day, there was a platform that had been built way out in the water. The only way to get out there was to be a good enough swimmer to be able to reach that far. There were slides on it, and you could dive off it. It was real attractive to the eye. I wanted to get to it, but it was really far. We're talking 'bout the ocean, y'all! The real deep! So I built up the nerve, and I set out for it. I made it out there with no problem. Oh, I was having a ball. Over and over, sliding and diving off it.*

*Now it was time to get back to the shore. I started going back and was doing fine at first. Then I began to realize that I was getting very tired. I guess I had used up a lot of energy out there from just playing around.*

*First my arms started going out. I couldn't reach anymore! Then my legs began to get weaker and weaker! I began to try to tread water to get a little rest! I could see the shore, and it was still far off in the distance! I wasn't going to make it!*

*Just lucky enough my father had gone out there with me. He came to my rescue! He wrapped my arms around his neck. I rode his back the rest of the way, and we made it back to shore!*

*Isn't that just like our heavenly father? No matter how far you get from him, he can pick you up and renew your strength. Allowing you to come back to him. He will never leave your side. He is your shore of life, your rock, and foundation.*

*I would have drowned without my father's help. You will drown without Jesus in your life. You don't want to get to far out in the world, out into the deep. Losing your life, marriage, or family. Stop playing out there. It's not worth it! Don't get to far from the shore!*

# IT'S TIME TO REMOVE YOUR FIG LEAVES

*Why are you hiding? Since the beginning of time, we've been trying to hide from the Lord. When Adam and Eve heard the sound of the Lord walking through the garden, they hid themselves. Oh, you know the story. They had eaten of the forbidden fruit, and now they knew they were naked. The Lord said, "Who told you that you were naked?" Before, they didn't even know that they were naked! Now when was the last time you went outside without clothes, not knowing you were naked! Couldn't God have made them knowledgeable enough to make them some clothes before their sin?*

*Instead they were free to roam the garden with no worries. They had total dominion over the earth. Only one command from the Lord. Not to eat of the tree of knowledge of good and evil. For on the day you eat of it, you shall die.*

*Now out of the whole Bible, there are so many stories, but this one I must say has to be one of the shortest. It took three chapters for God to create the whole earth, create man, and for man to fall. Think about that! The WHOLE EARTH! Then THE CREATION OF MAN! We blew it just as fast as God gave it to us!*

*In shame of this act, man tried to hide. Fear set in! Embarrassment set in! Deceit set in! Now they knew they were naked, and they wanted to hide themselves. Now they were fugitives running from the law!*

*They began to try to cover up their sin. We try to cover up our sins today. Layers on top of layers of lies and excuses. You can't hide from God. He sees all that you do.*

*It's time to get naked before the Lord. Take off those layers of the forbidden fruit. The evil thoughts, sexual immorality, theft, murder, adultery, greed, malice, deceit, lewdness, envy, slander, arrogance, and folly. Take off those clothes and wash 'em. They're pretty dirty! Repent!*

*It's Time To Remove Your Fig Leaves.*


# SINNER BREAKDOWN

*Drop the S and you have inner. We get caught up on the outside of ourselves that we don't realize that it's the inside of us that counts. You can be as clean as you want on the outside, but it's what's on the inside that devours man. Drop the S and work on your inner to breakdown a sinner.*

## CRUCIFIX

*On the cross of society*
*I stand before you naked*
*Arms stretched wide*

*I'm you everything from*
*Sex, drugs, and suicide*
*Took a walk through hell for eleven hours*
*Visions of pain and agony*

*You should be here, just look at your past*
*Is what the Devil whispered to me*

*Well, the twelfth hour fell*
*God snatched me from hell*
*And poof, now I'm here with you*


## DUTIES

*Are you running?*
*Are you scared of the duty of serving the Lord*


## PSALM 23 SAYS, THE LORD IS MY LIGHT AND MY SALVATION
**Whom shall I fear?**
**Psalm 91 says, he who dwells in the secret place of the most high**
**Shall see God**
*The enemy will try to trick you into believing that it's dangerous to serve God*
*The enemy's attack will come on you full force*
*When you are trying to establish God's kingdom*
*Because Satan knows what you will do to his kingdom…shut it down*

*So whose kingdom do you want to be a part of?*
*There's safety in the master's arms*

*There's evil in Satan's camp*

*Make a wise decision and choose your employer*
*I don't know about you, but I want to be hired by the Lord*
*I will carry out his duties until the day I die*
*For they that wait upon the Lord will renew their strength*
*And mount up with wings like eagles*

*For the unrighteous there are so many unnecessary consequences to pay for*

*So where do you want to work?*
*It's time to clock in!*


**THE CROSSOVER**
*When you cross the street, don't you look both ways?*
*When you hear the ringing of the railroad tracks, don't you stop and pay attention?*

*We need to do that every day.*
*When you walk out your front door, on one side there's righteousness.*
*On the other side, you have wickedness.*
*You make a choice every day, every hour, every minute*
*To cross on either side.*
*You make the choice to be a girl or a woman.*
*You make the choice to be a boy or a man.*
*Grow up*
*Stop murmuring and complaining*

*The people of Israel had to cross the Jordan River to make it to the promise land*
*To make it out of the wilderness.*
*Are you in the promise land*
*Or are you living in the wilderness*
*What do you need to crossover from?*

*Lying, stealing, cheating, fornication, adultery*
*It's time to crossover*
*Cleanse yourself*
*Just think about it*
*It's your life, and your body*
*No one can do it for you*
*Try Jesus and make the crossover*

## STAR

*When Jesus was born, a star marked where he was, and the wise men followed the star till they reached him. Have you ever thought about what they went through to reach the star? Or how far the journey was? Lack of sleep, maybe they ran out of water, and I'm sure a camel was not the most comfortable ride. In these days we have everything. Nice beds to sleep in, unlimited supply of water, and we can get anywhere quickly by plane, car, train, or by bus. And we are still lost. Instead of searching for our star, we are lost going through worldly issues. Your journey does not have to be so uncomfortable. **Proverbs 20:24 says, A man's steps are directed by the Lord. How then can anyone understand his own way?** The Lord wants us to live a prosperous life. We make the road bumping by our choices. If the Lord has given you instruction, follow through with it. Satan will try to get you off track. **Proverb 16:3 says, Commit to the Lord whatever you do and your plans will succeed.** So just as the three wise men pressed toward the mark, be patient, be relentless, and find the star.*

The more I read my Bible, the more the poetry just flowed from me. My mother was a prayer warrior, and she had had so many people praying for me across the country during the past few weeks. I had prayers covering me from coast to coast. One of the people that she had praying for me was Bishop Carlton Pearson. He was a very well-known minister from Tulsa, Oklahoma. My mother and Carlton had become friends when I was still in high school. Back then Carlton was one of the biggest, and most known, preachers you could find. His church, Higher Dimensions, was one of the first mega churches of its day.

My mother felt led to go to his church through Carlton's yearly Azusa Conference. The Azusa Conference was a very huge, weeklong conference that attracted believers from all across the globe. It was a big thing back then! So many ministries were born out of this conference.

After attending Azusa my mom decided that she wanted to actually join Higher Dimensions. Now keep in mind that this was about a hour and a half drive from Oklahoma City. I used to be like, "Momma, I'm not going to church every Sunday all the way to Tulsa."

She said, "Boy, you going!"

The church that we grew up in was only minutes away from our house, but now every Sunday we had to get up so early to start getting ready for church so we could be on time.

I hated the drive. I couldn't understand why we had to go that far just to go to church. Drive there and then after church have to drive that far home. I wasnt even the one driving, and I was doing all the complaining. Little did I know God was working on my behalf way back then. God had placed a star for my mother to reach just like my poem, and trust me, she reached it every Sunday for years! LOL! Although I hated the drive, once there I realized why my mom was lead. The power of God was there, and the anointing of God indeed took you to a Higher Dimension in your walk with the Lord.

My mother had told Carlton what I had done, and he helped keep her lifted up in prayer. He also sent her some tapes of some of his sermons for me to listen to and told her that he wanted to see me when I got out of the hospital. She gave me the tapes and told me that he wanted to see me. That alone empowered me even more to keep digging in my word. *The Bishop Carlton Pearson wants to see me*, I thought. *Little ole me!* I was just so grateful for someone that highly regarded wanted to see me. That week all I did was listen to Carlton's tapes on my headphones, and I kept praying and studying the word of God.

By the end of the week, we went to Higher Dimensions for service. Service was wonderful as always, and after service he had his staff escort me into his office, and we sat and waited for him. Carlton and his wife, Mrs. Gina, came in and greeted us all. He gave my mom a big hug and gave me one as well and told me, "Boy, get on in here and talk to me." We went into his private office, and we talked.

"So what's going on? What happened?" he asked. I began to tell him about all the pressure I felt I had been under and all the smoking and drinking that led to the confusion of my mind. He just sat there and listened to me. He asked me about my kids. He wanted to see what I had been writing about. So I let him see my poems. He read a few of them as I sat and eagerly waited for a response.

He stopped reading and looked at me and said, "You're preparing to speak." He told me it was like I was writing short sermons. He said God was going to place me in a position to speak and reach a lot of people! He told me that this was why God spared my life and that my testimony was going to help save more people than I would have ever imagined. *Am I gonna be a preacher or something?* I thought. I had no idea to what capacity or how I would be used, but to just know that I could help someone else encouraged me even more to keep going.

He prayed for me and over my life. We walked out of the office, and jokingly he said, "Ain't nothing wrong with that boy. God just about to use him that's all!" LOL! "That boy 'bout to speak to the people!" He began to pray for all of us as a family, and we said our good-byes.

The whole way back home from Tulsa, all I kept hearing in my mind was, "You're preparing to speak. You're preparing to speak." Wow! All this time really I was just writing for myself. I really didn't know that one day I would be sharing any of it with anyone besides my family. I begin to envision myself on stages in front of thousands of people. Could Carlton be right? Am I really preparing to speak?

To be continued…

Want to know what happened next? What do these pictures mean? All taken after my suicide attempt.

David shown with his sister Nerissa Berry alongside the CEO of The American Foundation for Suicide Prevention, Robert Gebbia and Vice President of Development and Field Management for AFSP, Michael F. Lamma

Kanye West with David and his mother Cheryl

David and Reverend Al Sharpton

David and his new addition Autumn Lily Threatt

Be on the lookout for the complete edition of *And Then I Woke Up, From Suicide to Success.* Available 2017 everywhere books are sold.

Author Contact/Booking Information

Facebook:www.facebook.com/andtheniwokeupinfo
Twitter: @Suicide2Success, @ThreattTweets
Instagram: Ahmadokc
Website: www.DavidThreatt.com

# About the Author

• • •

DAVID AHMAD THREATT IS A forty-two-year-old entrepreneur, father, and survivor of attempted suicide.

Born in Ancon, Panama Canal Zone, he was raised in Oklahoma City, Oklahoma. Threatt owns The Hair Café Barber Shop & Salon in Oklahoma City and is the chairman and founder of The American Foundation for Suicide Prevention (AFSP), Oklahoma Chapter.

Threatt has served as an Oklahoma state-appointed Suicide Prevention Council member since 2011. He received the Toast Masters International Communication Achievement Award in 2014 and was featured in The Huffington Post in 2015.